ROBERT SMITH ('NIGE')

THE TECHNICAL PROGRESSMAN

A DOCKYARD APPRENTICE WORKS HIS WAY UP

ROBERT SMITH ('NIGE')

THE TECHNICAL PROGRESSMAN

A DOCKYARD APPRENTICE WORKS HIS WAY UP

MEMOIRS
Cirencester

Published by Memoirs

1A The Wool Market, Cirencester, Gloucestershire, GL7 2PR
info@memoirsbooks.co.uk | www.memoirspublishing.com

First published in England, 2013

Book jacket design Ray Lipscombe

ISBN 978-1-86151-160-7

Printed in England

CONTENTS

DEDICATION

I dedicate this short account of my early adult working life in Chatham Dockyard (now the Historic Dockyard) to my ex-workmates and colleagues who have read my earlier book *A Dockyard Apprentice's Story* and said that they enjoyed that particular trip down memory lane. Their praise and encouragement has been most appreciated.

Given this unexpected reception, I now intend that this story of my experiences as a Technical Progressman will be the second in a trilogy detailing my Ministry of Defence employment. So don't forget - it's your fault for encouraging me!

INTRODUCTION

This story is a brief account of the first five years of my working life in Chatham Dockyard, shortly after completing my apprenticeship. Those earlier events were detailed in my first book, *A Dockyard Apprentice's Story*.

Having completed my apprenticeship training as an engine fitter and turner, I worked for a short while in the engineering factory as a fitter on turbine auxiliaries, before transferring to the Weapons Section to take up duties as a Technical Progressman. This book details those experiences.

CHAPTER 1

DECISIONS, DECISIONS

So this is it then? The apprenticeship is over at last. Five years of training and poor money, and now I am a fully qualified fitter and turner. The bee's knees.

Wrong. I was qualified, but I soon realized that only now would I start to learn, and a lot of experience was needed before I could consider myself a tradesman proper.

On completion of my apprenticeship I remained on Section 31 (Turbine Auxiliaries and Pumps) in the engineering factory for about 18 months. The major problem with this was that the work was drying up and patchy, and consisted mainly of refitting (overhauling) pumps for store (to be held in the Naval Stores until required for use by another ship or dockyard). This made it difficult to learn and improve my skills, and time hangs so heavily when there is little to keep you occupied. Worst of all was the need to look busy when visitors or managers came into the section, and the frustration at spending such a long time training and then finding no apparent end result. At this time I looked at leaving the Dockyard, as many of my contemporaries had, but I hesitated, as I was not sure that an engineering fitter was to be my long-term chosen career.

This feeling was probably prompted by working in a section consisting almost entirely of old men. The majority were 55-plus and most were over 60. To a 21-year-old this was almost antique!

For all sorts of reasons, including the hard times many had experienced during the war etc, they were not a happy lot, very rarely smiling, and had little or no conversation, personality, drive or enthusiasm. They seemed just grey automatons waiting for their retirement, or death. It was not the place to nurture future plans and ambitions.

The second most important reason why I was reluctant to seek other in-trade employment was that the majority of 'external' engineering works were mainly employing machinists. This usually meant 'minding' an automatic lathe or milling machine and succumbing to the daily grind of 'knocking out' millions of widgets (components), often working overtime to achieve decent wages, invariably on piecework (bonus), and in a dirty, noisy, and unpleasant environment. This did absolutely nothing to inspire me.

However, to change my life's direction and enter into a completely different vocation without any relevant qualifications was not going to be easy, so I stayed on section 31 and waited until something that promised a little more optimism for the future came along.

The life-changing event for me was a Vacancy Notice (VN), which appeared on the section's notice board. (This was the means of promulgating internal job vacancies.)

A vacancy had arisen in the Weapons (ships' armaments) Section Planning Office as a Technical Progressman (planning assistant) at the enhanced pay rate of 21 shillings per week.

I sought advice from my ex-skipper, Bob Nicholls, about applying for this job. His succinct advice was – 'Well, what have you got to lose?' That said it all really; nothing. So I applied for this job, went for the interview, and was successful.

CHAPTER 2

LEARNING THE ROPES

I reported for work at my new section on the appointed day and was directed to the Trade Office on the top floor of a new brick-built extension at the front of the weapons shop, where I was introduced to the Chargeman, Peter Lowry. We made our introductions, and Pete explained a few of the domestic arrangements - location of the toilets, clocking-on station etc. He said he would take me into the main office to make the introductions, but he stopped when he noticed that I was still wearing my normal work boots. He remarked 'You won't need those any more old son, we always wear shoes around the office.' I felt a little embarrassed, but grateful for the advice.

We went into the main office, known at that time as 'TO8' (Trade Office number 8), and Peter requested quiet. Then he announced: 'Can I have your attention please? We have a new starter, Bob Smith, and he will be working with Jack Payne.' Everyone in the office turned, nodded and said 'Welcome Bob'. A good start, and I felt at home.

The office was divided into two halves. On the left hand side were John Pattman, Jim Greenaway and Norman Shipley, who were the Estimators, supported by Ken Hancock and Fred Murr, the Technical Progressmen. On the other side of the office were Estimators Ron Hill and Jack Payne supported by two more Technical Progressmen, Bob Butler and now myself. Another Technical Progressman, without portfolio (although allegedly concerned with the introduction of the new Stage III Weapons Workshop), Keith Harris, completed the technical complement, and two Non-Technical Progressmen (Bill Allen and Ted Broadie) completed the staffing.

Outside the planning office a corridor led to the Inspector's office (Frank Stevens), the Library, run by Fred Ludlow, and a small room containing a wash basin and a toilet cubicle. At the end of the corridor was the Stock Control Office, run by Jack Taylor and two female assistants. This office held details of all major weapons equipments and major sub-assemblies, their location and their state of repair: serviceable, repairable, or currently being repaired.

The ground floor housed the Inspector's office (three staff) and the two Foremen's offices. One was for the shops (Main Shop, Annexe, and the Preservation and Packaging shop or PIP); the other Foreman was responsible for the 'Afloat' work (work that was carried out on board the ships). The main toilet block completed the ground floor accommodation.

Over the next few weeks I gradually got to explore the other parts of the section. These included the Weapons Annexe run by the Chargeman, Eric Carter, where compressors and hydraulic pumps were overhauled and tested. An old school-pal, Bob Webb, worked here, along with the other fitters, Bob Moncur, Lenny Price, Lenny Harris and a few others.

Next door was the PIP shop (Preservation and Industrial Packaging), run by the Chargeman, Phil Hobling, where large tanks of various steam-heated chemicals were used to clean components and assemblies, some to be returned to a refitting section, others fully preserved and packed for dispatch to the Naval Stores.

Phil Hobling was a lively character. He had been transferred from the Optical Shop near the Dockyard's Bull Nose when the work repairing ships' binoculars and sights had dwindled. Although he was near to retirement age he was very active, and always ready with a plethora of the latest jokes he had heard at his favourite watering hole, the Falcon Pub in Marlborough Road.

The main weapons shop itself was split into various sections. The main area was where the very large ships' main armament (4.5 inch guns) were refitted, along with various other smaller assemblies and equipments. This area was run by the Chargeman, Ned Foster.

At the end of the main shop were the dust-proof room and the section's small machine shop. The dust-proof room was where the more sensitive assemblies could be worked on in a clean and controlled area. Items such as the tachometric boxes were refitted here. These were a type of very simple mechanical computer which were used to control the gun mountings' movement and positioning. The machine shop had a small selection of machine tools, including a lathe, milling machine, a shaper and a drill, and was used to provide urgent and specialized machining support to the workshops; it was run by Harry Barnett.

To one side of the workshop was a small discrete area used by a couple of boilermakers who were attached to the section. They would manufacture or repair small to medium-sized items such as handrails, covers, machinery seatings and brackets and take details of any larger items which would then be manufactured in the main boilershop. At the head of the workshop were the naval stores (which stocked jointing, fastenings, and consumables, replacement overalls, and other day-to-day requirements) and with it was the loan tool store area. Next came the clocking station, the Trade Union representative's office (Fred Foster), a cloakroom and drying room area, and stairs which led to a mezzanine floor where the weapons equipment stores (spare parts and assemblies) were located (run by Len Parfitt).

Stairs at the far end of the workshop led to the Sight Gallery. This was primarily where the afloat gangs resided. Usually only one or two would be in the shop working on an assembly which had been removed from the ship. John 'Ginger' Peters was often to be found in this area, and he was known to be a very good contact if any engraving was required. John was highly skilled at engraving, and could provide work at least equal in quality to that provided by local sources; he was already engraving cups and trophies presented by the various dockyard sports sections. The Chargeman was a largish outgoing type called Ken 'Brockie' Brockwell.

Just outside the main workshop on the south side, a long single-storey building housed the diagnosticians. These were senior and highly-trained staff recruited from the workforce to undertake the various testing activities climaxing at the 'set to work' stage of the refits. Any major equipment was reliant on these teams to ensure that the equipment was fully operational and fit for purpose in every respect. They had their own special test equipment, and considerable technical literature complementing the section's Technical Library.

The workshop had a steady flow of work, and there was an upbeat feeling to the place. Most of the staff and workforce usually had a smile on their faces; it was a good place to work.

The section also ran a very active social club, so that's what Keith Harris did? I went on a couple of coach trips organized by the club, the first of which was to the Talk of the Town, where we saw the singer Frank Ifield. Some of the girls, including my girlfriend Joy, were devastated when they heard that Cliff Richard had been the headline act the week previously - poor old Frank didn't have the same appeal! However, he put on a good show, and it would have been a good night if our group hadn't been sitting close to an air conditioning unit which pumped out cold air all night. The food was fairly average too, and only just about warm by the time we were served.

The other main show I went to with the Social Club was at the Circus Tavern, just over the Thames in Essex. I can recall that we were all impressed by the size and décor of the venue, but again getting the meals out to the tables while the food was still hot proved to be impossible for the limited staff available. I can't remember who was playing at the show, so it can't have been very memorable.

Other events were organized by the Social Club committee, and these included 'Pitch and Putt' at the Mote Park in Maidstone and 'Bat and Trap' at the Five Bells in Church Street, Gillingham. These nights were usually good fun. Most of the managers would come along at some time or another and join in. Sometimes they even offered to buy us a pint!

The Social Club also ran a Premium Bonds club where all these members contributed five shillings (25p) each week, and were allocated bonds in return, about once a month. I've still got all my bonds, and I'm still waiting for them to present me with a decent prize!

Other trips organized by the Social Club were to the Theatre and the Shepherd Neame brewery in Faversham, which was for some unknown reason very popular!

The job itself, as a Technical Progressman, was obviously completely different to anything I had been used to up to that time. All of a sudden all my recently-used hands-on skills as a fitter were to be tucked away into the memory bank, while other attributes which had been dormant for so long had to be recalled. Much later on I was to look back at some of the earliest work I had done in my new job as a Progressman, and was amazed at my handwriting. It had not been used to any great degree for perhaps ten years, and not surprisingly it looked just like a schoolboy's.

At first everything was strange. Working in a new section, I soon discovered that a lot of the equipment we dealt with was referred to by acronyms; a close range blind fire director was known as a CRBFD, for instance. Then the myriad of forms, much loved by the MoD, and referred to by their numbers (rather than what they were for) had to be learned and remembered. For example S145a was a Stores Requisition, D83 a Stores Return Note, D387 a Special Demand Form, D1045 a Works Requisition Form, etc etc.

The next part of my education was to get to know where the work that was to be undertaken in the other (external) workshops would be done, and how to request it. Once the works request had been made, the requested completion date would be logged, to enable progress checks to be made. This would constitute a major part of my new job as a Progressman.

Sometimes, work completion updates would be arranged by telephone, backed up by written authority. These checks could be supplemented by workshop visits, which were often very interesting, and made the jobs come to life.

The major workshops visited for work progress updates were the Engineering Factory, the Boilershop and the Electrical Repair Workshops, while others included the Joiners/Patternmakers, Hose Shop, Coppersmiths and the Smithery/Chain Test areas.

In the Engineering Factory almost any machining operation could be carried out. The machine tools in this workshop included lathes (various types and sizes), milling machines, slotters, drilling machines, shapers and grinders, some of which were computer controlled. Workpieces could be shaped/manufactured to almost infinite combinations.

Various refitting sections overhauled all but the very largest shipborne equipment and water pressure testing, static/dynamic balancing, dimensional inspections, testing machines, both destructive and non-destructive, and a Tool Room were part of this comprehensive engineering facility.

Managers' offices (Inspectors and Foremen), Dimensional Inspection and the Trade Planning Offices were located at the North-East of the building. First line supervisors (the chargemen) had their offices co-located on their sections.

The Boilershop was a massive factory, second only in size to the engineering factory, with a large clock tower at its western end. It manufactured a wide variety of items from plate or bar steel (including some smaller boilers) and prefabricated sections/compartments for installation on board ships (funnels, lockers, racks, shelves, benches, trunking etc). Specialized brackets were made to drawings or in accordance with simple sketches as appropriate.

Various heat treatments (hardening, tempering etc) could be done using one of the several forges located in the workshop. The forges were mainly used to heat the workpieces to a 'soft' condition (red/white hot) which could then be hammered into the required shape.

Later on a massive hammer, previously located in the

Smithery and powered by steam, was installed in the Boilershop and converted to a pneumatic supply, to enable the forming of red-hot workpieces into large basic forgings.

The Electrical Repair Workshop specialized in the testing of new electric motors (prior to installation) and the overhaul and testing of in-service electric motors of all types and sizes, both AC and DC. Additionally all electrical components (control boxes, starters, solenoids, lighting and heating equipment and a diverse variety of associated items) could be refitted and tested in this workshop.

Other workshops included the Hose Shop, which would manufacture and test any hoses required for water, hydraulics, pneumatic, or steam services, as well as canvas and leather items if required.

The Smithery and Chain Test houses had provision to test chains, shackles, hawsers, metal and rope strops etc after manufacture or as part of a periodic test/inspection procedure. The Joiners/Patternmakers workshop provided repair capability for wooden furniture/fittings on board ship, and could manufacture new items from provided drawings. High quality and professional standard or bespoke furniture was manufactured in this workshop for use in the officers' quarters and wardrooms on board the ships. Top quality timber or occasionally veneered woods were crafted into intricate items and polished up to a mirror finish. Ships' and boats' badges were also manufactured as required in this workshop.

Finally, the Hydraulic Shop played a major role in the repair work in overhauling and testing of components and assemblies fitted in the ships' hydraulic systems, eg steering pumps and hydroplane equipment.

Another significant and important task of mine was to arrange work or materials from outside sources, known as 'direct local purchases' or 'special demands'. This would include things such as repairs or spares for specialist equipment not supplied through the Naval Stores system.

A walk through the Weapons sections was different each time as the refitting work was progressed and completed, and new and different equipment was brought in to take its place.

Walking through the main shop, you could always see one of the main ships' armaments (mountings, these are called), a massive 4.5 inch twin-barrelled gun, which always reminded me of an iceberg, as most of the working parts were under the gun itself, and on board ship would be located below deck. It would take many months to refit these mammoth pieces because of their complexity and the requirement to test each sub-assembly before and after installation.

Fred Whale was the leading light on this equipment, with his mate Les Taylor. Fred was quite a character. One of his unusual habits used to manifest itself whilst he was talking to one of the other workmen in the shop. While he was talking very rapidly and enthusiastically he would undo all the buttons on the front of this person's overalls and then do them up again, without apparently realizing he was doing it!

The other large items in the main shop were the ships'

directors. This is the equipment which controls the guns and positions them onto their targets. At this time mechanically-operated directors were still being used, the common one for the main armaments being the Mk 6M; these were usually refitted by Peter Castle.

This was the main equipment of my concern. I found the work very interesting, especially as I got on well with Pete, and I felt we made a good team. I also established a good working relationship with the Drawing Office, and over a short period of time was able to secure a complete set of the latest issue of working drawings (I estimate about 1000 in the set).

Routine day-to-day tasks would comprise arranging overhauls or testing of the sub equipments (often in the Hydraulic Shop), the manufacture of components (usually in the Engineering Factory), arranging plating (or other protective coatings such as painting or anodizing) and purchase of 'special' equipment.

I was also allocated the task of compiling the 'Monthly Letter', which was the list of all the equipments being worked on in the section, showing their state of progress. This was used as the basis for the routine planning review meetings.

The Technical Library was an essential asset to the section. It held updated copies of the Navy's 'bibles' (Books of Reference or BRs as they were known). These contained all the technical and administrative information required in the operation of a naval establishment.

Held additionally were technical reference books covering

all the topics necessary, including such information as specifications for materials, bearings, fastenings, protective coatings, oils and lubricants, heat treatments etc. A major and vital part of the technical library service was to ensure that all the information was kept up to date with the latest amendments. This was critical to ensuring that when the equipment left the section it was always updated to the latest specification, and all the literature held in the Library was referred to and treated as 'controlled' for this reason.

Other equipment being refitted would normally include 40mm Bofors guns, which could be battery (Mk 8), electrical (Mk 9) or more usually the hydraulically-operated (Mk 7) version. There were also 20mm Oerlikon guns, which were mainly used in anti-aircraft or close-range defence roles.

Like most offices, the work would at times be hectic, sometimes boring. One particular Friday lunchtime will, I'm sure, stay in all of our memory banks forever.

It had been a very busy morning, with all of the chargemen wanting urgent stores or materials (which they had mostly forgotten) for the weekend overtime working. The panic over, things went quiet about ten to twelve, and we all puffed out our cheeks and took a deep breath. After a few minutes Freddie Murr on the other side of the office was absent-mindedly 'pinging' his rule on his desk in time to a subconscious melody. After a few seconds, someone on our side of the office picked up the beat by gently banging their knee against the side panel of their desk.

Next to enter this orchestral treat were two guys humming

and one da-da-da-ing, each tapping out a rhythm with their knuckles on their desks. The icing on this particular cake was when the chargeman (Pete Lowry) started to prance down the central aisle in the office playing an imaginary trombone with enormous gusto. Pete was a big fella and was carrying more than a little too much weight, and he invariably had a comical air about him. This looked like a scene straight out of the Jungle Book. The whole office was now really rocking. I don't know what the tune was, but it was of a good generous tempo and progressively increasing in volume!

At the height of this orchestral masterpiece, the Inspector (Frank Stevens) walked in and was hit by a wall of sound. He stopped a yard inside the door, rooted to the spot, mouth open and a look of monumental surprise on his face. The 'music' tapered off quite quickly and Frank recovered his composure (just). He glared at Pete Lowry and said 'What the hell's going on in here? It sounds like a bloody bear garden!' With that, he spun on his heel and left, slamming the door on the way out. Complete silence. Then Pete Lowry started to giggle, and the whole office collapsed into uncontrollable mirth. We were all concerned that Pete would be in trouble and be reprimanded, but he later assured us all that there were no (apparent) repercussions.

I consider myself lucky that I was transferred into the Weapons section at this time, as the Management, and in particular the Trade Office Inspector (Frank Stevens, my Line Manager), were very progressive (certainly ahead of the game) in terms of staff development. In two key areas they led the way compared to all the other sections in the Dockyard at this time.

Firstly, almost all of the equipment we worked on was covered by excellent training courses at one of the Navy's 'schools' at Portsmouth, HMS *Sultan*, HMS *Excellent*, HMS *Dolphin* etc, and we were strongly encouraged to attend these. Secondly, Frank Stevens ran lectures and classes to prepare any staff interested in advancement by taking the MOD Navy sponsored examination papers. This was in preparation to sit the 'Inspector of Trades' Examination which was held every two years, sponsored by the Navy Department. This examination was the normal and preferred promotion route into middle and senior management. At that time people would not only be sitting the exam from the Home Dockyards (Chatham, Devonport, Portsmouth and Rosyth) but also from naval bases/establishments worldwide (we still had some then!) including Malta, Gibraltar, Singapore and many others.

Frank held classes after work one night a week when we were set homework and could discuss last week's topics and problems on a group basis and pool information.

The essential requirement to enter these study sessions was to obtain a copy of the naval engineering 'Bible', BR (Book of Reference) 3003 Part 2. This was not a restricted publication, and could be purchased at places like W H Smiths. I obtained my copy second hand from my pal Bob Webb.

The bottom line was that the Management on this section gave every encouragement to any staff who showed an interest in promotion or advancement, and most of us went on and got at least one or two promotions. These results could be traced back directly to the encouragement and assistance given to us by our forward-looking line managers.

CHAPTER 3

BACK TO SCHOOL

The 'Pompey' courses were legendary, not so much for the technical expertise acquired, which was considerable as most of the course Tutors were ex Chief WEAs (Weapons Engineering Artificer), or similar, therefore highly experienced and knowledgeable, but because of the students. Usually at least two students would attend from the same dockyard on each course, and several courses could be running simultaneously. Therefore four, five or six men from Chatham would often be attending courses at the same time.

The preferred lodgings were with Mrs Simmonds in Salisbury Road, Southsea. This was mainly because the food was not only excellent but also importantly these "digs" were cheaper than elsewhere. At this time course attendees were given a daily allowance, and if you found really cheap digs, it left you with more beer money! I even know of people (not from Chatham) who slept in their cars (and were moved on several times by police during the night) so that they could save the money they had claimed for lodgings! Incidentally, by about mid-week these people had started to look more than a little frayed at the edges!

Mrs Simmonds would usually start the week giving her guests

enormous food portions and gradually reduce these over the week until by going home time the portion sizes were just about right. The sleeping accommodation was, let's say, adequate, usually two or three beds in a room, and very basic. These sleeping arrangements were never a problem though, as it was only a place to 'crash down' after a night out, usually involving drinking.

Another incentive for staying with Mrs Simmonds was that she was rumoured to have two very attractive daughters, so there was always the possibility that you might get lucky! All in all Mrs Simmonds was the place to lodge, and you had to get your booking in early, as the word soon got out and the guys from the other dockyards would try to book in there as well.

The Portsmouth weapons courses, as previously explained, were very professionally run. The instructors were usually senior NCOs (Chief Petty Officer or equivalent) and they had many years experience working with and maintaining the equipment they taught. They knew the kit backwards.

The courses themselves supplemented the theoretical lectures with the opportunity to get 'hands-on', stripping the equipment, re-assembling it and doing any tests that were required. Special emphasis was given to fault finding and modifications. Practical and written tests were included during and at the end of all courses. If you wanted to learn and had even the slightest intelligence, you would find these courses invaluable.

The various training establishments, HMS *Sultan*, *Excellent*, *Vernon*, *Dolphin* and others, had excellent facilities, decent classrooms, test/training rigs and video and projection equipment, and all courses provided stationery items and comprehensive 'hand out' notes to be taken away and retained for future reference.

I attended most of the courses on offer, but one in particular I shall never forget. The course was in the winter 1965/66 at HMS *Excellent*, to be instructed on a gun directional system. Two other guys from Chatham, Bob Moncur and Trevor Sargent, went with me. I would take the other two with me in my car, a trusty Wolseley model 15/50, registration VEL 797, a number plate I find easy to remember. I was nominated to drive as Bob had a two-seater, and Trevor didn't drive.

The journey down to Portsmouth and the first two days of the course were fairly routine - course, pub, bed, course, pub, bed - but Wednesday nights were always a bit special and something to look forward to - the 'Widows' Hop' at the Mecca.

On this particular Wednesday we met up with two of the other Chatham guys, Ted Coward and Brian Turner, who were in Portsmouth on different courses and staying at different 'digs'. While Ted and Brian decided to display their dancing skills (sensible chaps), Bob and I decided to display our drinking prowess (Bob was ex-Merchant Navy, and loved a drink or three!)

We were quite happy drinking our chosen poison for the evening (pints of Double Diamond with Pernod chasers), and about 9.30 we bumped into the chief who was our course instructor (Chief O. A. Fair). He said we were obviously having a good night and asked us what we were drinking. Double Diamond with Pernod chasers, we told him.

'Bloody hell, you'll be ill in the morning', he said. 'Whadya mean?' we replied (far too stupid and drunk to take advice). 'We're roughie-toughies, not soft like you wimpy sailors.' He was right; we did suffer for it next morning, and how!

In the meantime we carried on drinking, and shortly afterwards when I came back from another trip to the toilet, Bob had company. I don't mean to be rude, but this woman was *ugly*. That's not very nice I know, but her face was dominated by an enormous nose, hooked like a witch's but so wide it looked as if someone had thrown a bunch of sausages at her face and they had stuck!

I feared for Bob, because I was convinced that if she turned her head sharply this enormous conk would decapitate him. However, shortly after I returned she decided to leave and I had the opportunity to quiz Bob on what had happened. Apparently as soon as I got up to go to the toilet she had targeted Bob and sat down at our table. With very little preamble she had asked him if he wanted a 'good time' (They could go to a hotel she knew of not far off). When Bob politely declined, she then offered a 'knee-trembler' quickie in the alley alongside the dance hall, which would cost thirty bob (£1.50). Again Bob said thanks but no thanks, so her parting shot was 'OK then, how's about I give you a quick wank under the table for ten bob?' By this time I was on my way back to the table, and she had spotted more likely prospects elsewhere.

At the evening's end we made our way back to Salisbury Road unmolested, but drunk as skunks. Next morning was a nightmare. I had the grandfather of a hangover and suicide seemed the only sensible option. At breakfast Mrs Simmonds produced the usual full English before I could stop her, sausage, bacon, eggs, mushrooms and tomatoes glaring at me from the plate and daring me to try them. The smell that wafted up around my greenish face induced almost uncontrollable waves of nausea. If I hadn't known Mrs Simmonds better I would have sworn that she was a sadist.

On her return to the breakfast room she saw the breakfast untouched, and I had to explain that I didn't feel too well. The breakfast disappeared in a flash (boy, was I grateful) but almost immediately (or so it seemed) it was replaced by a large plate of scrambled eggs. Oh dear! I sat there. This was indeed a test of wills. Could I outstare the scrambled eggs?

They remained in place, untouched, and perhaps ten minutes later Mrs Simmonds removed them, to my utmost relief! I don't think my mumbled apologies were fully understood.

On to 'class' then, and to try to get through the day without (a) vomiting over all and sundry, or (b) dying from acute alcoholic poisoning and its best friend the hangover from hell.

The morning passed agonizingly slowly. The Chief Instructor thought our condition was most amusing, and made a big play of slamming down desk lids at every opportunity, and an even bigger play of offering us headache cures, which we accepted. He said, quite rightly, that we had been warned that our drinking exploits would come back to haunt us, and how right he was. Somehow I made it through the morning session, and by lunchtime I was feeling much better; I thought I might live, and started to feel hungry. The other classmates said they were off to a local fish and chip shop which they knew to be very good, and this sounded fine to me.

We got to the 'chippy' and placed our orders. Mine was a large cod and chips (by this time I was starving) and I waited, salivating. My enormous fish and chips were eventually placed in front of me, and boy did it look good! Was I going to enjoy this!

Well no, I wasn't. As soon as I lifted the batter off my lovely piece of fish and the smell wafted up around my nose, a violent feeling of imminent nausea attacked me and I had to bolt for the door. I wasn't sick, but there was no way that I was going to be able to eat just yet. That would teach me, I wouldn't be drinking any more. Well, not until the evening!

During the afternoon session we had to change classrooms to work on some training equipment across the site. As we walked through the 'school' along by the water the Chief looked at the sky (which was a strange colour) and said ' Just look at that sky, we'll have some snow tomorrow'. We all laughed, as it wasn't that cold. We should have known better; he was right.

We decided, Bob Moncur, Trev and I, that we ought to have a quiet night out on Thursday. We had been told by one of the lads who was on a different course (Freddy Kimmings) that the place to go for a good night out and the chance to meet some attractive women was the Joker Club. This was a small nightclub in the centre of town which offered various types of gambling.

When we went out for the evening we didn't intend to visit the club, but as the evening wore on, a few beers later it seemed like a good idea. In fact, a very good idea.

Incidentally quite a few of the Portsmouth/Southsea pubs were tied to the Brickwoods Brewery at this time, and this was a brew to avoid at all costs as far as most of the Chatham lads were concerned. Quite early on in our visits to Portsmouth we had found Brickwoods ales to be disgusting. In fact we had a contest to see who could drink the most. We lined up a pint each along the bar of this pub, and the winner would be the one who could drink their pint first, or drink the most out of their pint. Bear in mind that amongst us were the notorious 'Beer-Pigs' from Chatham, and they would drink anything. Well not on that night. I think the winner in this particular contest drunk less than three quarters of his pint, and we were amazed at his fortitude in being able to do this! That beer was horrible. The nearest anyone came to explaining its taste was that it was like lukewarm cat's sick and coffee. Not even the King of the Beer Pigs, Ted Robinson, could swallow this Brickwoods' beer, so it must have been really bad.

Incidentally, Ted was another of the amazing characters about at that time. When we went on a course with him he would invariably chase us all up after our evening meal, which we usually had together, so that we could get out on our drinking session with him in good time. It was usually a bit of a struggle getting out in a hurry, as we were full to the gunnels with Mrs Simmonds' evening meal and felt completely bloated. This never seemed to deter Ted however, and we would all be chased out to the pub selected to start our evening's pleasures. This was when the first problem started, because as the landlord pulled up the pints Ted would invariably take one of the first ones, and before the last was pulled he would have drunk his and would say: 'come on then, gee up, who's for another?' We would look woundedly at each other and try to keep up. After about four pints at this pace some of us (me included) would go on to 'halves' but we still couldn't keep up!

One incident, often recalled, was classic Ted. A group of us were walking 'home' (back to Southsea) from a good night out in town, and as we made our way along the seafront we were passing the boating lake when a completely rubbish drunken discussion reached its high point. Ted said 'It's a matter of willpower, mind over matter, and I'll prove it to you.'

With that he sat down, removed his socks and shoes, rolled up his trouser legs and clambered over a dwarf wall into the (shallow) end of the boating lake. 'I'll show you what I mean' he said, and prepared to walk into the lake. 'What's he doing?' someone asked.

It appeared that Ted was going to walk ON the water across the lake as a demonstration of his willpower! One of the guys, I believe it was Jim O'Kane, was trying to reason with him, but of course by now it was a matter of pride.

Ted got about four feet into the lake (on the bottom, not on top of the water) when a passing police patrol car happened by. When they had been appraised of the situation, they looked at us, rather sympathetically I thought, and told us to 'bugger off home'. Good advice. We did.

So on this Thursday night we had our 'few beers' (not

Brickwoods) and headed off towards the Joker night club. The night itself was strictly routine. We had a couple of drinks (half pint bottles and quite expensive), and spent a couple of pounds each at the card tables, without really having a clue as what to do. Trev was quite smitten by one of the croupiers, but then again Trev was convinced that most of the female population were in love with him anyway. Bob and I had decided by about 11 pm that we were not going to 'pull', as we thought the girls in the club were not likely to be very interested in a couple of almost skint dockyard mateys.

Trev, however, had other thoughts. He had somehow persuaded a croupier that he fancied to let him walk her home. He told us that she finished work in about 15 minutes, lived quite near, and her 'pad' was on our route walking home. Would we wait for him and we could all walk that way together?

A reasonable request, so that's what we did. When the girl finished her shift we all left together and walked back towards Southsea. We arrived at the place where the girl lived, said goodnight, left Trev to see the girl to her door and made our way back to Salisbury Road and our most welcome beds.

Next morning at breakfast we asked Trev if everything was all right (by this time he was usually deeply in love and talking about getting engaged, or some other rubbish) but he was not over-enthusiastic in his replies. So she hadn't found her one true love overnight?

We did ask Trev 'How did you get to take such a gorgeous dolly bird like that home? Did you resort to your usual bullshit and tell her you were a wealthy playboy or something?'

He gave us his best little-boy-lost look and said he might possibly have exaggerated a little on one or two comments he had made to her.

'Like what?' we asked.

'Well, I may have let slip that I have a new sports car, that my mum and dad are very wealthy and I'm an only child.'

We had to smile. We knew Trev could spin a good yarn (as with most of us on a good day), but no harm done. Or so we thought.

At mid morning the Navy has a tea/coffee/cigarette break, known as a 'stand easy'. Just prior to stand easy on this Friday morning a naval rating knocked on the door of our lecture room and told the Chief (Instructor) that Chief Petty Officer Smith was to report to the Lieutenant (known in naval parlance as Jimmie the One) at stand easy. Our instructor told the rating that this class was all civilians, so he should try elsewhere. We had our stand easy, and forgot about the incident.

Shortly after stand easy the rating appeared again, and told the Chief that 'Mr Smith' was required to report to the Lieutenant immediately. Uproar amongst the class members, and I left to seek out 'Jimmy the One'. I was escorted to the Lieutenants' Office by the rating. I knocked and entered.

The lieutenant introduced himself, we shook hands, and he asked me to sit down. He then explained that he found himself in a very awkward situation, and would like my help. I had no idea what he was talking about, but said that I would certainly help if I could.

He then asked me if I had been to the Joker last night with some friends. When I answered 'Yes', he dropped the bombshell. He explained: 'I know that you are not directly involved, but we have received a telephone call this morning accusing one of the party you were with last night of attempted rape.'

Rape? I couldn't believe it. Apparently the girl could remember my name, and was accusing one of the group I was with.

The Lieutenant asked if I knew who the person in question might be, and if so would I get them to contact him immediately. The girl had threatened to go to the (civil) police if she had not heard from the lieutenant, and received an apology, by twelve o'clock (noon). The lieutenant also asked if any of 'my party' was injured as the girl had stated that when she tried to ward off her attacker she had hit him with a large piece of timber!

To say that I was livid was probably the understatement of the year. I got Trev out of the classroom and told him sort it out with the Lieutenant NOW. I didn't even think to ask him what had happened, although I was almost certain that there was no complaint to answer; explanations could come later.

It was all sorted before lunch. The lieutenant didn't give us chapter and verse, but piecing together what we did know, and what we were told, it seems likely that the girl had decided to try her luck with a spot of blackmail.

Trev had tried to impress the girl and had told her that he had very wealthy parents who had just brought him a nice new sports car for his birthday and that they lived in a great big house on the coast in Kent, etc etc. It was thought that this was most likely the trigger for the blackmail attempt. During the course of the discussion with the Lieutenant, the girl said several times that she wished to keep this news from the papers and his parents, but that would depend upon circumstances.

It transpired that when investigations were made this was not the first time that this sort of incident had occurred with the same girl involved. Trev was told there was no case to answer and he was free to go. Whew! Lessons learnt there!

It had started snowing on Friday morning (just as the Chief had said), soon after eight o'clock, and by ten o'clock there was four inches of snow everywhere. The Establishment had been monitoring the worsening weather reports, and decided that all courses would finish by noon at the latest. By this time another two inches of snow had fallen, so now it was six inches deep and still falling!

We left HMS *Excellent* at 12 noon, and immediately hit the kerb outside the 'School' gate, as the snow was already so deep that we could not distinguish the path from the road. The first job was to find a filling station and top up with petrol. This was when we realized just how cold it was. I could not open the flap above the petrol filler cap as the lock had frozen solid. I used my cigarette lighter to heat up the key, and after several attempts the key went in, unlocked the cap, and I could fill up.

The next problem was seeing through the windscreen. Our breath was condensing on the inside of the glass and immediately freezing up! (The car heater was fairly primitive, and could not cope.) Luckily, or perhaps by planning, I had a gallon can of anti-freeze in the boot when I managed to get it unlocked, and we used this to cover the outside and inside of the windscreen, and even used a duster soaked in anti-freeze to keep my glasses clear!

We also took advantage of this stop to take extra (dirty) clothes out of our cases and put them on over the top of those that we were wearing, to try to keep ourselves warm.

So we started the torturous route back home. There was no A3(M) or M27 then, and EVERYBODY was trying to get home. We, like everybody else, could not make any speed because the roads were so congested and still covered in ice and snow - bloody dangerous. We crawled along the A27 at a snail's pace. It was still very cold, and the only good news was that it wasn't snowing quite as hard. Every time we came to a standstill, usually after just a few yards, it was difficult to start again, as the car just slipped on the ice and slid down the camber into the kerb. When the tyre came up against the kerb it would find sufficient traction to move on a few more yards, provided it was just a gentle tweak on the throttle.

By about 10 pm it seemed we had been travelling forever, but we had only reached the outskirts of Brighton. We could see a large roundabout up ahead, which was causing the latest hold-up. It looked like a scene from an old war film! All the cars had ground to a halt, and people had got out of their cars to exchange experiences.

In the car behind us was a young woman with two children.

When we got out of the car to investigate this latest hold up, she did the same. She told us that she was very concerned that her husband would be worrying where she was as she had left Portsmouth at one o'clock. No mobile 'phones in those days.

We told her that we had left before her, so she had done very well; also we tried to reassure her about her husband's concerns, as all the radio news stations had told people what was happening.

After we had been at this spot for about ten minutes the traffic still showed no signs of moving. We were all so hungry that Trev decided he would try to find a nearby pub, before they closed, to get something to eat; crisps or chocolate perhaps? We were starving.

Trev disappeared with our caution in his ears not to be too long, as Murphy's Law dictated that as soon as he went the traffic would start to move again and we would have to go without him! Our luck held for once and he made it back to the car, armed with chocolate and crisps, just before the traffic started moving again. We shared our chocolate and crisps with the woman and children in the car behind. She was delighted, and you should have seen the kids' faces.

The rest of the journey home from Brighton, once we were clear of this wretched roundabout, was slow, but after what we had experienced all day it was almost a treat. There had not been the same extremely heavy snowfalls we had had in Hampshire, and by now a lot of travellers had managed to make it home safely, so the roads were not so crowded. We arrived back in Medway exhausted, really cold, and really, really fed up, at about half past one on Saturday morning.

Trev lived in Whitstable, so there was no way he would be able to get home that night (or to be correct, morning as it was now). Bob offered to put him up at his place in Gillingham, and the offer was gratefully accepted. Trev's real complaint, and one which he had been wittering on about for practically the whole journey home, was that he would not be home in time for his mate's stag party on Friday night. Some chance! We had been enjoying the pleasures of being stuck in a snow-bound A27 somewhere near Brighton when all the frivolities were taking place.

I dropped Trev and Bob off in Gillingham and hurried home to my rented house in Ingle Road, Chatham. I was in a hurry to get home, not only because I was knackered, hungry, and thirsty after the nightmare journey back but because for the last hour I had been really desperate for a poop!

Home at last, I dashed through the house to our outside privy, and sat down feeling grateful, relieved, and content with the world! Heaven! No light in this toilet, of course, and suddenly I felt rather cold and wet. Looking upwards, I could see the stars! As my eyes adjusted to the gloom I could see that a big hole had appeared in the toilet roof; obviously several tiles had gone missing, and the toilet floor now had a nice new carpet - of snow. I didn't linger, having completed the job.

This trip did have a happy ending though, as the Dockyard finance department ultimately paid us the 14 hours travelling time it took us to get back! Almost unheard of, as they were usually really mean bastards.

That course was the most memorable for all sorts of reasons, but almost all the courses seemed to provide at least one incident which was memorable in its own right, and usually hilarious, at least at the time. Another incident quickly comes to mind, again involving Ted Robinson, beer-drinker extraordinaire. I was staying at Mrs Simmons', as usual, and sharing a bedroom with Keith 'Porky' Harris. We had all had our evening meal, had our wash and scrub-up and changed into our 'fanny-trapping suits', and stinking of Old Spice aftershave we were in the downstairs lounge watching TV, while waiting for Ted to finish his ablutions and join us.

We were making polite conversation with Mrs Simmons and more importantly her two very tasty daughters, while sussing out any remote chance with either/both of them, when suddenly all hell let loose. An anguished shout was quickly followed by some very heavy crash-bangs, and very colourful swearing. It was BANG, SCRAPE, CRASH, then 'Fuck it!' and 'Bollocks!'

We all rushed out into the hallway and there before us was a truly wonderful sight to behold. Ted, rushing from the bathroom in just his bathrobe, had slipped at the top of the stairs and fallen down the lot. Our first concern was that he might have badly injured himself, as it was a long way to fall, top to bottom, but our concern was short lived as we saw the spectacle before us.

Ted was lying at the bottom of the stairs in a sort of star shape, his legs pointing upstairs. His hair was all over his face, and his gingerish beard was wet and straggly, 'Jesus Christ!' he shouted, although to us he looked more like Rasputin, on a very bad day. His white bathrobe had been pulled open, and as he laid there his 'tackle and two' (which was indeed a frightening spectacle) was exposed to all and sundry.

We (the boys) all giggled. They (the girls) went sort of wide-eyed, rushed to his aid, and sought his reassurance that nothing was broken. I noticed that their eyes did flick down several times to check on the 'family jewels', and remained there just too long before Ted had adjusted his dress.

Was it me, or did I afterwards notice that Mrs Simmons could sometimes be seen with a fond smile on her face when looking at Ted, and he also seemed to get even bigger dinner portions after this occurrence?

It may sound as if the courses at Portsmouth were all play, and not much attention was given to our studies, but nothing could be further from the truth. The fact is that a group of young lads away from home will usually find entertainment of some sort to keep themselves amused, and this usually involves drinking and women. However, we were all very grateful for the opportunity to attend these excellent instructional courses; we studied hard and gained the maximum benefit from them. I can't remember anyone failing the end of course exams and tests. We took this expertise back to our parent shipyards, and were the better skilled because of it.

CHAPTER 4

PROGRESSMAN'S PROGRESS

After about eighteen months in the new job I felt I had mastered most of the new skills required as Technical Progressman, and was really enjoying the work. Most of my colleagues were young (of a similar age to myself) or at least had a young outlook. A lot of the time I was given the autonomy to improve the technical assistance I could provide by obtaining excellent technical publications such as the 'Adspec 1110' which catalogued all ball and roller bearings held within the naval Stores (this was thousands), with a brief description of their recommended application (how and where they should be used).

I soon became the Section's 'expert' and could advise on the application and quality of the bearings, usually by interpretation of the dot-marking system. The Adspec also cross-referenced to the Army and RAF supply chains, so we were able to obtain items from those if necessary.

Another excellent guide was BR1336/68; this was the reference which covered the multitude of oils and greases which were held, or could be supplied through the stores system, and the use for which they were designed. Very handy when oil types were superseded or changed.

The time passed very quickly, due in no small part to the job satisfaction which I felt, as I was able to see that partly by the results of my efforts the tasks in the workshops had been progressed or completed. I enjoyed the work, and because I enjoyed it, I was good at it. I did not realize at the time that this was being noticed. However, I did make the odd mistake, and one in particular led to a serious 'piss-take' from my colleagues. I was asked to order 30 pairs of pipe-clips for the 40mm gun mounting, from the Pattern Shop. Somehow in the 'denomination' box (the type of number required, eg single, dozen or hundred) I managed to put SET instead of PAIR. A set in this case was 24 pairs, so I had ordered 24 times the quantity required!

Christ, when they arrived there were pipe-clips everywhere, and didn't my mates let me know it. 'How's the Pattern Shop Nige, still on night-shift knocking out your pipe-clips?'

Well, I certainly learnt a lesson on that one, and was very careful with the 'denomination' box on demands after that.

At about this time, eighteen months into the job, Bob Butler retired. He sat on the next desk to me, and was the very experienced Submarine Technical Progressman. I was asked if I would like to assist and provide cover for these duties for the Submarine Section, or more correctly the Submarine Weapons Section. This was a very good sign, as this was one of the most demanding and important jobs in the office. It was a sure sign that I was considered to be competent in my duties, and to have the potential for advancement.

I jumped at the chance to take on this new high-profile challenge as I looked forward to learning the new equipment and managerial skills which I would require, albeit on a relief-cover basis. I was certain that I would do a good job in this area, which would provide the platform for future promotion.

I had a week's familiarization with Bob, so that he could explain the distinct skills and contacts that would be required in these duties. Bob was a serious sort of individual, ex Navy, but very knowledgeable and conscientious. He helped me all that he could in the handover period.

The Submarine Section equipment was different for lots of reasons. For example:

- Most of the equipment was in direct contact with salt water, so different materials were often used (phosphor-bronze, aluminium-bronze, gunmetal and naval brasses etc.), all with varying degrees of anti-corrosion qualities.
- One of the first major tasks was to replace some of the major assemblies with the latest specification of bronze, as a result of extensive trials and problems encountered.
- Some of the equipment would need to be subjected to high test pressures, pressures which would be encountered when the submarine was submerged and at depth.
- As the torpedo tubes were the main armament of the submarine, they were considered to be 'critical equipment'.
- The equipment was more often affected by modifications and was updated constantly.

- Torpedo tube equipment usually had a bearing on the 'integrity of the hull'; therefore it was seen as key equipment and subject to special testing and safety requirements.
- Most planned work done on the torpedo equipment was undertaken using material lists.

This was an excellent document, used mainly when major refits or complicated modifications were to be carried out, produced by the Drawing Office. They usually accompanied a set of engineering drawings, and tabulated the item number, drawing reference, item description, number required and source of supply. This would be shown as the NATO Stock Number (NSN) or if not a 'patternised' item (an item supplied through the naval stores system). It would also be the authority to purchase from local suppliers.

The work would require regular inspection/progress visits to the submarine being refitted, which I always found to be extremely interesting. This is not to say that I would have liked to go to sea in a submarine, or even to work as an engineer on board for an extended period, as the extremely cramped conditions had to be seen to be believed!

I always found that in general the ships' and boats' crews (surface and submarine), got on extremely well with the dockyard repair teams, although this was obviously in both parties' main interests; it was more than this. I believe it was a relationship brought about by mutual respect, and I feel that this bond was the strongest with the dockyard repair teams and the submarine crews.

Time seemed to pass very quickly, and soon we had a visit by one of our old colleagues, Bob Moncur, who had been transferred on promotion to RNAD (an armament depot) at Coulport in Scotland, about three months earlier. Bob was always the one with a biting wit, and the way he told a story, with a deadpan expression and not the hint of a smile, would have us all in stitches.

We asked him how he got on with his posting, and as near as I can remember this was his reply. He said that the first major difference he noticed was the weather. If we thought the weather was bad 'down south', we should think again (Bob had been transferred in late September, so it was winter weather he was experiencing). He said that it felt as if it had not stopped raining since he had arrived in Scotland, and usually the rain was accompanied by a biting cold wind. This situation was made even worse by time of year, which meant that the days were so short and it barely seemed to get light most days. He thought Coulport was a dark and depressing town, so not much to cheer you up really.

His first day at work was a revelation. After the routine 'signing-in', issuing of a gate pass and the other usual domestic/administrative arrangements, he was introduced to his new boss and they embarked on a workshop tour. They entered a large workshop with two rows of benches running along the whole length, with workmen working on opposite sides. The workshop was obviously quite old and the first thing that struck Bob was that the lighting should be improved. Then the noise; not machinery but the unmistakable sound of hammering on metallic objects.

As they approached the first bench Bob could see, to his

horror, that a workman was hitting a very large brass-cased ammunition shell with a big lead hammer. Boy, was he giving it some stick! Bob stiffened, backed away and very nearly shat himself. He looked at the supervisor wide-eyed and open mouthed, and was met with a paternal smile. 'It's perfectly safe', he was told. 'All necessary safety measures are taken, and at this stage the ammunition is not in an active state.' Yeah? Well, it still took some getting used to!

As time went by Bob became more comfortable in his new working environment, and lost the background feeling that Armageddon was just around the corner. His principal task was to produce a time estimate to complete the various activities in the Armament Depot. This was work he enjoyed, having been doing similar work in the naval Base at Chatham, and he was fully experienced in time and motion procedures and the many other skills and practices required in the management of bonus payment schemes.

The other thing that helped Bob was that he felt that the work practices at Chatham were far more advanced than those at Coulport, which he considered to be somewhat behind in the way they conducted their business.

The social life in this part of Scotland at that time did not impress Bob. The pubs were men-only, dingy establishments where the natives were far from friendly. If spoken to they tended to scowl back and reply in an often incomprehensible broad Scots dialect. Up until that time he had not encountered any attempts to make friends, or even friendly conversation, by the locals.

Bob's 'digs' were not the best either. The Personnel Department had arranged his accommodation, so that when he reported for duty the first time he would have a pre-arranged place to stay. He was booked in to stay with an elderly widow-lady in the older part of the town. Bob described her as at least eighty years old, but very sprightly. She looked (unfair to say, but perfectly true) exactly like the wicked witch in *The Wizard of Oz*, dressed always in black from head to foot. She rarely spoke except to complain.

She provided an evening meal as part of the arrangement, but the food was impossible to identify, and although the colour varied very slightly the taste (or lack of it) did not.

He occupied the 'box' bedroom. This he was told, had previously been occupied by the landlady's son when he had lived at home, and as he had probably left home some fifty years earlier, at least, the room didn't look as if it had been decorated since. You get the picture, don't you?

All of the above paled into insignificance however, by comparison with the cold. The lodgings were a Victorian two-up, two-down terraced house, which was small and had no heat retention at all. It was dark and damp and had no central heating or double-glazing. After the evening meal, a couple of hours could be spent in the 'living room' where the tiny black and white television would be showing the soaps and programmes of the landlady's choice. This was the only room in the place that had a fire lit on a regular basis.

If you can picture this scene: a small dark room, the

centrepiece a tiny coal fire which seemed to produce little more heat that a torch bulb. In pride of place, directly in front of the fire was the landlady's cat, always. The landlady sat in her chair directly in front of the fire, and Bob would be sneaking a view from the side! He could often see the fire, although he never actually felt it. It was about this time that Bob realized just how frugal the landlady was in her spending habits.

Bob did not stay in these digs for very long, and his reason for leaving was a little unusual. One night things were as always: small fire flickering away, cat curled up in front of it, landlady dozing fitfully. Another night filled with fun and frivolity was in store. Suddenly a commotion was heard in the street outside, with a bell ringing and lots of shouting. Neither Bob nor the landlady made any quick move to investigate, as of course if you moved you would surrender your place in the pecking order near the fire.

Suddenly: disaster. There was a sound of rushing water and almost immediately the whole room was enveloped in a massive cloud of soot. Bob, shocked, looked across the room, but could only just make out a pair of eyes, wide open and startled, through the billowing soot clouds. He heard, rather than saw, the cat dashing around the room in panic, trying to locate the door. It eventually found its way out, and was believed to be last seen streaking towards Glasgow.

Apparently a fire in next door's chimney had been reported to the fire brigade, and these guys had turned up looking like an excerpt from an old black and white movie with an antique fire tender and part-time volunteer firemen. When they arrived it was obviously very dark, although several neighbours had braved the cold, made it into the street and were now milling around panicking.

The lead fireman had made the roof-top, but in his excitement he had placed the water hose down the wrong chimney – Bob's lodgings. It took some little while before the mistake was recognized, by which time the hose had flooded the wrong house, and the original chimney fire had put itself out.

We were all helpless with laughter when Bob recounted this story to us in his inimitable and hilarious fashion, and tongue-in-cheek we accused him of starting the fire so that he would have a good excuse to change his digs. Anyway, he did change his digs, and ended up in far more civilized accommodation.

Bob settled down in the new job, and now that he had nice accommodation, things were looking up. After a while he (almost) got used to the wretched weather. He used to say that in Coulport it had just stopped raining, it was raining, or it was about to rain; usually the middle one.

He did come back to Chatham to visit friends and relatives still in the area, and usually made a point of calling in to the Dockyard to see us on the Weapons Section. We always enjoyed his visits, his hilarious story-telling and the news from north of the border.

CHAPTER 5

DOWN THE PUB

The social scene at this time was great, although of course at the time we did not appreciate it. Mainly our social lives centred on pubs, but what pubs they were! In your early twenties, the world is your oyster. If only we could have realized it!

One of my best friends at this time was Ted Arnold, who lived in Upchurch, and his local was the Brown Jug. He used to "force" me to go there with him, and we had some great Friday and Saturday nights there. This pub was something else, you really should have been there, for you would have enjoyed it as much as we did.

Several things combine to make a good pub, but the main one in the case of the Jug was that the Landlord, Eric Funnel, was fairly young but very experienced, and really did know how to run a pub. He had a very outgoing personality, fully supported his darts and euchre (a card game) teams, and was always looking for ways to improve the entertainment value of his pub. He and his wife Pat made an excellent team. No wonder that eventually they were among the longest serving publicans in Kent, if not the longest.

The other main ingredient of a successful pub is the

customers. What a load of characters this lot were. We won't see the likes of them again.

One of the most notable of these characters was 'Schubert', so called because of his penchant for playing classical music on the old piano in the back bar. Schubert was a Scot, obviously well educated, and it was strongly rumoured that he came from a very wealthy and well-connected family in Scotland, who gave him a regular 'allowance' as long as he (the black sheep of the family) promised to stay away.

His piano playing was a bit of a problem. Early evening, 6.30-7 pm, he would play quite nicely, but he would then start his drinking. This was usually a 'Final Selection' (a very strong bottled beer), followed by a large scotch whisky chaser. After a few of these, usually by about nine o'clock, the piano playing was loud and awful. Les Dawson wasn't in it. Eric would normally appear at this stage and tell him it was time to go home, often with the inducement of one for the road.

One night when Schubert was in especially fine form and roaring drunk, most of the pub turned out to see him leave. He used to drive a large old black Vauxhall, and on this night it wouldn't start. One of the lads offered to help and opened up the bonnet of the car. 'You'd better come and look at this' he suggested to the interested group that had gathered, me included. Underneath the bonnet there was a gallon jerry can wired in place above the carburettor. This was Schubert's petrol tank, and it was empty. To cut a long story short, when he realized he had run out of petrol, Schubert fell out of the car, staggered to the boot, retrieved another gallon can and filled up. We all stood well back, in case the whole lot exploded.

Back in the car, he started up and lurched off up the road, leaving clouds of dense smoke in his wake. Fifty yards up the road he nudged the bank on the nearside of the road and veered violently across to the opposite side, glancing a telegraph pole and putting (another) dent in his front wing. Completely undeterred, he continued on his way the short distance to the houseboat which was his home. Luckily this was only about half a mile from the pub, but heaven help anyone who met him coming from the other direction.

Quite often at weekends some of the locals would get together in an impromptu music session. George Chaney was one of the leading lights in this, and he would bring his guitar or banjo to entertain us. One of the other locals used to keep time with a 'kerdonker'. This was a large weighted boot with a long broom handle secured inside and sticking upwards. All around the handle were nails loosely holding metal beer-bottle tops so that they were allowed to move against each other and make a jingling sound. This was accompanied by the rhythmic thumping of the boot onto the pub floor, keeping in time with the music.

The leading light in these singsong sessions was usually Freddie Kimmings, often supported by his brother and/or sister. I had known Fred ever since our primary school days, and he had always been the life and soul of the party. He had a vast repertoire of drinking songs, and knew most of the current pop stuff as well, and would break into song at the drop of a hat. He loved to sing, and he *really* loved his beer. Often when the pub closed, Fred would dash out to his car and return with a couple of empty five-litre plastic containers which he would get Eric the landlord to fill up with 'Master Brew' beer to take home for supper.

Freddie was a character in his own right, and it used to amaze us lads how he got away with running two long-term girlfriends, each knowing about and apparently accepting the other. This was not even a short-term situation, but one which lasted for years. He had set nights which were allocated to his girls, and they normally shared weekends!

Phoebe was Eric's mum, usually known as Fag Ash Lil. She lived with Pat and Eric at the pub, and loved to play in the card schools, especially euchre, at which she excelled. Sunday night was usually the big cards night, and often five or six tables would be busy all evening.

I have cause to remember one Sunday night euchre session very well because it was highly embarrassing for me (afterwards).

One of the couples that used to visit the pub regularly on a Sunday for the cards was Pete and Margaret from Maidstone. On this particular night Ted and I were partners playing euchre against Phoebe and Margaret. After about ten minutes into the session I was struck by an acute case of wind. This was bad enough, but I had been drinking Guinness the previous evening, and had had a massive curry for dinner. Well, the inevitable happened and I farted. Not the honest-to-goodness type, which says 'here I am'; no, this was the carpet slipper type, the very spiteful kind. I had had a couple of pints during the course of the evening anyway, and was feeling pleasantly at peace with the world. Well, it swelled up around us, an unseen cloak of pernicious fart. I couldn't help myself; I had this delicious feeling that my fart would at any second strike with enormous effect.

The first one came and went unnoticed. I searched for clues - any signs of distress/panic amongst the others? Nothing. Well, maybe a slight reaction. I thought I had seen Phoebe blink, and Ted's nose twitch.

All this time I was fighting like buggery to stop myself giggling and standing up, arms aloft, and shouting 'It's mine, It's mine, all mine!'

The second one was a real beauty, even if I say so myself. It crept out with such panache that I knew it was in a class of its own. Suddenly Phoebe stood up and glared at all of us around the table.

'Jesus Christ, who's is that?' she demanded 'Someone's arsehole's on fire!'

The game was up. My faraway look of extreme pride and pleasure was replaced by uncontrollable giggles. Tears down cheeks. A memory to savour!

It's funny how one's attitude to farts can change. My pal Ted used to say that when he was first married and his wife farted he would say 'Never mind, darling, naughty pooper!'

After about a year or so of being married, if she did it again he would go all wrinkly-lipped and snarl: 'Stop that you dirty cow, before you shit yourself!' Perhaps an indication that romance was dead?

Landlord Eric was always ready to organize; often on a Saturday night at about ten o'clock he would ask if anyone wanted fish and chips. If there were sufficient takers, and there usually were, he would head off to the chippy in Newington with a shipping order. When he got back the pub would 'shut down' for twenty minutes or so while all and sundry scoffed their fish and chips.

One episode which happened about this time concerned a trip to the coast to go cockling (collect cockles). This was organized after a chance remark late on a Saturday night; not always a good idea. The tide was out early next morning, so it meant an early start from the pub.

A Mini Van was made available, loaded with the necessary crates of beer and off they went. At lunchtime Eric produced rolls, and proceeded to fill them with cheese which he had provided. Everybody tucked in except one of the lads, who steadfastly refused anything to eat at all. They all thought that perhaps he felt a little queasy after last night's boozing; it wasn't until much later that he explained that immediately prior to Eric doing the cheese rolls, he had been spotted having a shit, and no one saw him wash his hands! Anyway, no-one seemed to have any ill effects, either from the cockles or from the landlord's lack of hygiene.

One Friday night as we were leaving the pub, Ted's neighbour Whispering Reg Smith, who I had not met before, asked if we would give him a lift home. I had no problem with this as I was taking Ted there anyway. When we got to Ted's a very unsteady Reg got out of the car and asked what he owed me for the lift home. I said that I did not want any money as I was going that way anyway. Reg then turned very abusive and loud (hence the name, probably). He put his hand in his pocket, threw a handful of money into the car, told me to fuck off several times, slammed the car door and wandered off. This apparently, was his party piece. Ted later explained that Reg was well known in the road for his exploits.

For example, on one occasion Lyn (Ted's wife) was woken up about five o'clock in the morning by the reflection of a roaring fire in the bedroom window. Worried in case the house was on fire, Lyn jumped out of bed and stared out of the window. Looking across into Reg's garden next door she could see Reg's wife doing the washing in a galvanized tin bath over an open fire. This was the fire Lyn had seen. When Lyn talked to her neighbour some time later, she explained that Reg had spent all their housekeeping money on drink, and as a result their gas had been disconnected, so this was the only way she was able to do their washing. She was doing it at night as she was too embarrassed to let neighbours see her doing this during the day.

It certainly wasn't easy for Lyn's neighbour. She had a particular dread of Christmas as Reg liked to celebrate (even more than usual) at this time of year, and last year had been a disaster. He had been out at lunchtime on Christmas Eve, and had a skinful. When he got home after lunch he started drinking again, and by early evening he was with the fairies.

At about 8.30 there was a knock on the door. It was a

Salvation Army soldier collecting for the charity and preaching the message concerning the demon drink. Reg was so impressed with the Salvation Army guy that he invited him in and listened intently. Suddenly Reg saw the light, realized the error of his ways and was determined to do something about it. With the Salvation Army man's encouragement and help, all of Reg's Christmas (and other) drinks were emptied down the drain-Halleluiah! Halleluiah!

Next morning when Reg went to get his 'livener', he discovered that every single drop of booze that had been in the house last night had gone down the drain. He could not remember anything about this. To say that he was not amused doesn't even come near. His wife got all the blame and a good pasting for not stopping him from destroying his booze.

Another local at the Jug was Old Jack; in fact he lived in. He was another character, dry humour, shortish, tubby, usually wearing a waistcoat and a trilby hat. He was believed to be Phoebe's boyfriend. One night Eric served Phoebe a Cherry B, as she had expressed a wish to try a different drink. Eric said, as a throwaway line, 'You had better watch those Mum, they are pretty potent'. Jack, standing at the end of the bar, looked over the top of his glasses and sneered 'Be careful? Those Cherry B's are gnat's piss, they won't hurt you, unless you drink a pint of them'.

Eric took the bait. 'Gnat's piss, are they? Well I bet you can't drink a pint of them. If you drink it, I'll pay for it.'

So the challenge was on. Eric got a pint glass, poured four Cherry Bs into it and gave it to Jack. 'There you go then' he said, 'get that down your neck - if you're man enough!'

Red rag to a bull. Jack knocked back over half of the glass's contents in one go, paused and smacked his lips. 'Go on then, get on with it', was Eric's instruction.

Jack emptied the glass, banged it on the counter and surveyed the watching on-lookers with a barely concealed sense of pride. 'Told you, gnat's piss' he volunteered.

Several minutes later Jack went quiet, and his face went a funny colour. It wasn't red, more of a deep plum colour. He looked around the bar with a slightly confused look on his face, then gently slid down the bar and collapsed into a heap in the corner, unconscious.

Eric was the first to react. 'Gnat's piss eh?' he asked. 'Will some of you old boys give me a hand to put this twat to bed?' They did, and Jack was quiet for a couple of days.

Another great pub was the Three Tuns. This was my local more than the Jug really, in terms of being at the bottom of the road in which I lived, and it took over as our place to go for a drink once the drink and drive regulations started to bite. I used the 'Tuns' intermittently over quite a few years, and this pub also had its crazy characters and several landlords during this time.

The first landlord I remember was Old Charlie, a larger-than-life character who loved his darts team. Several weeks after I moved into the village (Lower Halstow) we visited the pub for the first time. Everyone seemed reasonably friendly and it looked as if it was going to be a normal evening until about 10.30, when Charlie burst through the door carrying a very large darts trophy which they had just won. Obviously flushed with the momentous achievement by his darts team (and a good few Scotch whiskies I guess), he lit the place up. Everyone was told to refill their glasses to toast the magnificent success of the darts team, and the place was instantly buzzing.

At around 11.15 we were about to leave when we were challenged by Charlie. 'What's up, don't you like my beer?' he asked, engaging the top bolt on the front door. A little sheepish, I replied that I thought eleven o'clock was closing time, and we were expected to leave. 'Don't upset yourself, old son, we don't worry too much about that sort of thing down here', he explained patiently. So we had another, actually a few more, and got home about half past one. I thought – I could get to like this place!

Friday night was always a busy night in the Tuns. Sometimes forty guys would be packed into the public bar. A dozen or so were jobbing builders, and loads of work was discussed, offered and arranged in between joke-telling sessions and lots of heavy drinking.

One of the regulars was a legend for his success with the ladies. He would often arrange to meet one of his special 'girlfriends' half way through the evening, when he would go missing for about an hour or so. On at least two occasions his wife telephoned the pub and demanded to speak to him, as she had a pretty good idea what was going on. When this happened the landlady would get one of his mates to answer the phone and tell his wife he had just gone to the toilet. This didn't really convince the wife, and she insisted that they got him to phone back in the next ten minutes. One of his mates would then dash up to the lay-by alongside a nearby orchard, and when the violent rocking of the car stopped, he would tap on the window and explain the emergency. The stud would re-enter the bar, make a wonderfully imaginative call to his wife, and all would be well - until the next time.

This guy was not overly discreet and his stories would entertain and fill us with jealousy in equal measures, on a regular basis. Initially we thought most of the escapades were products of his very fertile imagination. However, many of us would bump into him, usually in an out-of-the-way pub with different women, none of them his wife, and all of them good lookers. Mind you he did have the necessary requirements for his 'hobby'. He had the time, the inclination (oh yes!) and the money, as he ran his own company.

He was of course, not the only playboy in the village. In fact it seemed that at this time about 90% of the Friday night drinking school were having a bit on the side - or at least they said they did, or were working on it.

Not all the extra-marital escapades were confined to the customer's side of the bar. The old landlord, Charlie, had retired and one of several younger couples who had subsequently taken over were running the pub. Of course the landlord heard most of the tales from the opposite side of the bar, and he decided that he ought to take advantage of any opportunities that might come his way. I know he made up a foursome on several occasions with the aforementioned village stud, and no doubt a good time was had by all, but I remember one night was quite extraordinary, and far more memorable to me than all the others put together.

On this particular night the landlord had been out with some of his mates to a party, having left his wife and the barmaid in charge for the evening. He got back to the pub after midnight, drunk as a skunk. The landlady had excused herself about half an hour earlier, probably anticipating her husband's condition, and left the barmaid to see the few regulars off the property and to lock up. When the landlord got back he did not appear to want his customers to rush off home - in fact he served more drinks to those who asked and had one himself. He had obviously had a very good evening, was full of himself, and started flirting with the barmaid.

At this point it should be explained that she was a little on the plain side, but quite well built and a good sport. Well, one thing led to another, and it was easy to see what was on the landlord's mind. After making a blanket enquiry if anyone wanted another drink, he asked the barmaid if she would help him to find a brewery invoice in the back room. Off they went.

Between the public bar and the back room there was a small glass partition or serving hatch which was never used, and with large cordial and mixer bottles in front of it was never cleaned and largely forgotten about. Certainly the landlord had forgotten about it! One of the drinking party crept around the bar and peeped through. 'Christ, you'd better have a look at this' he whispered, waving us around the bar to spy through the hatch.

What a picture! The landlord had his trousers and pants

down around his ankles and the barmaid was bent over the table, skirt up around her waist. The landlord had his cock in hand and was manoeuvring, grunting and pushing and trying to get John Thomas home.

At last, success. She whimpered 'That's it, that's great, now fuck me to a standstill!' Like he needed any more encouragement! He might have been pissed, but Christ wasn't he randy! She obviously knew what she wanted, and now the opportunity had presented itself.

I must admit the sex scene being played out before us was quite a turn on (for me) but I had sensed the others moving away and when I looked round I saw why.

While the landlord was playing his little cameo role saying 'I warned you what would happen if I caught you serving late drinks', and thrusting like there was no tomorrow, the barmaid in turn was whimpering 'Yes, I know I'm naughty, I deserve it, punish me with that big hard cock!' Dear oh dear! Very theatrical.

I then realized that there was further movement alongside me and that two of the other customers were pumping the spirit optics for all they were worth. Several glasses were filled up with at least trebles, and either drunk down in one go or passed onto the bar for their mates. I would estimate that in the next ten minutes, half a bottle of rum and at least the same of brandy was swallowed without touching the sides.

The barmaid reappeared first, rather chirpy I thought, and started to make 'Don't you have homes to go to?' noises. The landlord did 'surface' before we left, looking a little sheepish, but with a significant smile on his face. It looked like a job well done.

A regular at the pub at this time, and a long term village resident, was Les Jones. Les was a larger-than-life character who lit the place up when he entered the bar.
During this period Les was mostly working at the Bowater paper works in Gillingham as a maintenance fitter, and this meant that all week he would be visiting the many different sections in the factory, picking up new jokes for his impressive repertoire. On Friday nights in particular Les would keep us entertained for hours, without repeating a joke once.

Les and I were also regulars at the Lower Halstow Working Man's Club, which was originally built for the recreation of the Eastwoods brickfield workers and located in an oast house-style building at the end of Westfield cottages.

There were again, so many characters that frequented this club, including Ray Cheyney, the Singing Shepherd (he usually gave us 'Old Shep' — bloody depressing); Bernie the Bolt, whose blue song repertoire included Bollocking Bill the Sailor etc, and Karen, the Beer Queen. She was immaculately dressed and turned out, but usually pissed by closing time.

Some of Les' relatives were also regulars (the village was almost incestuous at this time) and one of his sisters-in-law would occasionally come out with a greeting which intrigued us all. Apparently when Les was first married, he lived in a tiny, damp cottage in the centre of the village, which has long since been demolished. He was an enthusiastic and very competent sportsman, and played rugby, football and cricket at a high level. One Sunday morning he was late changing into his cricket gear, and the top drawer of his chest of drawers (where his sports kit was kept) was stuck due to the damp. He wrenched the drawer open and removed his kit, then tried to push the drawer closed with his hip. The drawer didn't move, so in frustration he gave it another full-on shove with his pelvis. This time the drawer slammed shut, trapping his cock inside!

He said he could not begin to describe the pain, and his anguished shouts could probably be heard in Upchurch, the next village! Picture him, eyes watering, standing on tip-toe. He had released himself by the time that his wife (Emmy) had reached the bedroom, coming up the stairs two at a time, but his cock had taken an awful battering. It was black, blue and throbbing!

No long-term damage was done; Les even got to the cricket match, but said that he was walking like a saddle-sore cowboy for a couple of days. He also volunteered that he was a little cautious when he put the 'old man' back to work for the first time shortly after his accident. Emmy was sworn to secrecy regarding the mishap, but of course she subsequently revealed all the sordid details to her sister.

Some months later, Les's sister-in-law had an accident involving the sash-cord windows in the back bedroom of her cottage. She was trying to open the window, which had jammed, by pushing upwards with both hands and with her body close in to the bottom half. Suddenly the sash cord broke and the top half of the window came down like a portcullis, trapping her dress and pinching her left breast into the frame. Her distressed shouts were heard, and she was quickly released by her shocked husband, luckily sustaining only nasty bruising, grazing and soreness. Subsequent offers and attempts to massage the affected area, and anywhere else for that matter, were supposedly refused.

Having been made aware of the background as above, it was now simple to recognize the reasoning behind the 'party-piece' greetings:

'Hello there, cock-in-the-drawer, how's things?'

'Fine, tit-in-the-window, how are you?'

Les was a smashing fella, and we became good friends.

Most of the social scene at this time was centred on the pubs. The most memorable nights happened when my mates were home on leave, and we could meet up for a Saturday night out on the town. Pete Barnes was in the RAF, Derek Hawkes was in the Navy, Richard (Dood) Hicks (my nephew) was at University (London School of Economics), and I (the 'fourth musketeer') was a dockyard matey. A diverse collection, we probably hadn't seen each other for several weeks, so there was plenty to talk about.

We were young, good looking and had a few bob in our pockets, so it was look out Medway, here we come! We could almost taste the anticipation of a good night out. Usually we would catch the bus from Rainham to Luton Arches in Chatham. The plan was to have a pint in all the pubs we liked (which was most of them) along the high street, going into Rochester High Street and along to Star Hill. Some chance! It must have been about two miles, and at this time I would guess that there were about thirty pubs along this route. Most are gone now unfortunately, but the ones I remember as our favourites were (starting from Luton Arches end) the East End

Hotel, the Coachmakers' Arms, the White Lion, the Fountain, the Duchess of Edinburgh, the Red Lion, the Sun Hotel (the Sunshades), the Von Alton, the Royal Exchange, the Rose and Crown, the Ship Inn, the North Foreland and the Hare and Hounds, although we never got that far without cheating and missing out a few! (Apologies to the other pubs I have missed out, if they are still there!)

The Duchess of Edinburgh and the Fountain always struck me as being quite lively, and here it was even more of an incentive to behave, as fighting often broke out and usually some of the working girls would be present (not fighting, offering their services).

Looking back it was all fairly tame stuff by today's standards. Most of the pubs were quiet early on, and we could hop from pub to pub, have our pints (most of which were pretty ordinary as I recall) and on to the next boozer. It was going home that sobered us up.

We didn't have money for taxis, so if we missed the last bus, which we invariably did, it was the long walk home. Rainham was only about four miles, but that can be a long way if it starts to rain, or the weather decides to deteriorate, and of course we didn't wear anything on top of our suits. If we had any money left we would sometimes visit the coffee stall in Railway Street for a steak and kidney pie (with plenty of brown sauce) and a cup of tea, plenty of sugar. Oh yes, we knew how to live!

The other main activity walking home (where we always expected to meet up with four gorgeous girls who were looking to meet up with the men of their dreams (us), and seduce us repeatedly, in spite of pleas for mercy) was 'hedge hopping'. For the uninitiated, this basically means running alongside a hedge (plenty of these along Watling Street) until you have built up enough speed to enable you to jump into the top of the hedge, which cushions your fall (hopefully). My problem with this was that the other guys had more than one suit, whereas I didn't. After a couple of jumps into the hedge I realized what was happening to my suit (how would I attract the crumpet without it?) and decided that hedge–hopping was not for me.

Chatham and Rochester were the places to go for the best entertainment. Most of the pubs were lively at the weekend, and there were so many in those days that we were spoilt for choice!

One of my favourite pubs at this time was the Rose and Crown opposite Grays' motorbike showroom at the Rochester end of the High Street. Usually on Saturday nights the pub would be full of darts players, several of whom were Irish lads who were building the M2 motorway, and Saturday nights they were out for a good drink, to let off steam, and an evening of darts. This pub was also a good base for an evening tour (pub crawl) and an ideal meeting place if a night at Victor Silvester's Dance Hall above the Gaumont Cinema at Star Hill was planned. This was where Dood would try to persuade us to go, as he had always fancied himself as a good ballroom dancer, and the answer to many a maiden's prayer to boot!

One such evening amuses me when I think back. Dood was on a summer break from university and was working at the Metal

Box Factory in Strood to raise some funds. This provided the bonus opportunity to meet a lot of the girls that worked on the factory shop-floor, and at this time he was courting one called Joyce. Joyce was a good looker, blond bouffant hair, nice make up, and legs which ran all the way up to her bum before they got cheeky (the old jokes are the best…)

This particular night Joyce was sitting opposite me, wearing a very mini mini-skirt, and I was joke telling, as usual. She had by this time sunk several Cherry Bs. The joke involved was the old chestnut about "If you cut a flea's legs off it goes stone deaf", and I was explaining this with appropriate hand actions. Unfortunately, as I acted out the joke, the cigarette I was smoking brushed against Joyce's knee and laddered her tights.

'You silly bugger!' she announced. 'Look what you've done to my tights!' She pulled up her mini-skirt to show us the extent of the damage, not realizing (or perhaps she did?) that she was giving half the pub a splendid view of her wonderful assets. Dood blushed, and wished that she hadn't explained quite so well; we were amazed and delighted. She became a firm favourite of all the pub from that day on. Boy, what a view!

On the dancing theme, another haunt of ours was the 'Pav', the Pavilion Ballroom, Gillingham. I don't really know why we went there except that there probably wasn't anywhere else to go. I think the Pav was really a training centre for the Samaritans. You could go out on a Saturday night, have a few beers with the lads and end up in the Pav, and that's when depression would set in - in a big way. I had been to lots of dance halls around the country, but never had I seen such a collection of ugly women assembled together at the same time. Not all of them of course, but a significant number, and certainly enough to terrify a young man. Not only that, but they invariably seemed to take great pleasure in refusing to dance when politely asked (I think this was probably one of the few thrills they got).

Dood, of course, loved the Pav, as it gave him the opportunity to demonstrate his dancing prowess, and of course he took his own 'bird', who happened to be Joyce. After persistent pleading from all the lads to bring some of her friends from the Metal Box factory as blind dates for us lads, he came up trumps; well sort of. He got Joyce to bring one of her friends with her.

That was the good news. The bad news was that she made most of the women at the Pav seem almost average. This one was never going to be called a looker. Of course, she latched onto me, and as the evening wore on she became less ugly, passable even - in the dark. To cut a long story short, she pestered me all evening to take her home. As a throwaway line I said I had left my motorbike at home as I would be drinking, so if she would like to walk home to Rainham with me to collect my bike I would give her a lift home! Ha ha, that should stop her persistent requests.

Well, no. Of course she said yes – in fact she jumped at the chance. (I thought afterwards that it was only marginally less distance to walk to Rainham than for her to walk home to Strood). At the evening's end I walked home and she tagged along. As we made our way alongside the Orchards in Lower

Gillingham I did consider suggesting that we hop over the fence and stop for a monumental roger, but by this time I had sobered up somewhat, and although I was drunk, I wasn't that drunk. (This was a major failing on my part, I was always too fussy.)

We eventually got to the bottom of my road in Rainham and I suddenly realized that I wasn't keen on this girl knowing exactly where I lived. I explained that I would need a while to get the bike out and start it up, so I was going to go on ahead. I dashed off. Bloody hell, I couldn't half run when I had to. I got the bike out and met the girl half way down the road. I took her home to Strood (still in the suit, no helmet etc) and dropped her off, refusing the offer of coffee, as this would have been dangerous. Also by now it was gone two o'clock and I was knackered. It was bloody cold going home on the bike, but at least I had escaped relatively unscathed!

I must admit that I did see her a couple of times afterwards, to make up a foursome with Dood and Joyce, but only when it was very dark. It was never going to be a long term thing.

CHAPTER 6

ONWARDS AND UPWARDS

I had by now settled in to my new duties on the section, and was enjoying it. The fact that the target dates we were working to were realistic and important, especially regarding the overhaul of the submarines, provided a high degree of job satisfaction. The people I was working with, the production team, the Design Division (drawing office), the contractors, and the support trades which manufactured or supplied the enormous amount of sub assemblies and equipments, were without exception, keen and dedicated to their work.

The other major bonus of working on the submarines was that due to its importance, correct and updated information was usually available. All equipment fitted on board was scrupulously monitored for defects (pre-installation testing), and updated to the latest specification, and complete and updated records were mandatory.

Configuration control (the 'standard' use of equipment and its location in a batch of ships or submarines) was a system which was preferred on surface ships, but was much more stringently controlled on submarines. The important reasons for this were:

- If a submarine on patrol experienced a failure on any of its equipment, and the necessary spares were not available on board, it was essential that the correct spares were supplied and that they would fit exactly into the space vacated by the defective items. This was to minimize downtime and ensure the correct performance of the replacement item.
- This system enabled the supply system, the Naval Stores, to ensure that it purchased only the correct spares required, and that they were to the latest specification and modification state.
- Configuration control could play an important role in reducing 'noise shorts'. This is basically ensuring that all equipment is fitted with the proper resilient mountings, and that it is not located close enough to vibrate against other equipment or a bulkhead. Noise shorts are a critical factor in silent running for submarines, and the British subs at this time had an excellent and well-deserved reputation in this procedure.

An important element in the submarine overhauls was ensuring that the latest issue of engineering drawings were supplied and used for the refit. These would show any modifications necessary to improve the efficiency and reliability of the boat, or would reflect some other essential change required. At least two sets of drawings would be issued to the planning office prior to the boat's refit starting; one set for the production team, as working copies, and one set to be kept in the Technical Library for replacements or for perusal by Production Management.

Both sets of drawings would usually be accompanied by a

material list, which as previously explained would list any associated drawings required; items to be manufactured locally (in the Dockyard); items to be sourced from contractor supply; any protective finish that was required to the components, eg heat treatments, chrome plating or galvanizing; and any other information considered to be relevant which would be required during the refit.

I believed I had established a good rapport with the guys in the drawing office, and found that if approached properly, they were more than happy to provide additional drawings, quite often very quickly, and would obtain additional technical data if this was required. I think that at this stage of my working life, my enthusiastic attitude and determination to do a good job was recognized and appreciated by colleagues and work contacts alike, and helped me become recognized as an asset to the section, and one to watch for the future.

On-board visits to the submarines were sometimes requested by the Production Inspectors. These were always very interesting, as you could see exactly where the equipment was installed, and get a real feel for how your efforts in the refit fitted into the grand scheme of things. Additionally, you could get an insight into the difficulty the production boys had squeezing all this equipment into the space provided - and of course it had to work, after it had been installed! It is quite impressive to see the compartments on board the submarines packed with all the equipment necessary for its self-contained patrols.

Apart from the main and secondary propulsion systems -

engines, usually diesel or electric - systems included fresh and salt water, refrigeration, air conditioning, hydraulics, HP and LP air systems, electrical power and lighting, navigational, weapons, galley equipment, officers and crew's quarters, and much more which had to be cramped in somewhere. Bearing in mind that British submarines are much smaller than surface craft, you begin to see what an achievement this is.

The on-board visits were always very interesting, but at the same time it was always good to get back to the office environment, to get warm and to escape the feeling of claustrophobia.

The submarines tended to be docked where the specialist shore supplies were available; this was in No 3 or 4 Dock, in the South Yard area, or more likely 6 or 7 dock (south of Basin 1). Progress update visits were also made to the main production workshops before the regular monthly Planning and Progress review meetings. This was a good opportunity to establish working contacts with my 'opposite numbers', the Progressmen, and also the line managers at these production centres, which were providing the required support effort for the equipment being refitted.

The Engineering Factory was probably the biggest support centre for our refit programmes. Almost any metal object could be manufactured in this massive workshop. The usual output was pipework flanges, pump shafts and impellors, special nuts and bolts and engine parts, along with practically anything else that was required.

Almost all the normal materials were machined in this workshop, including the ferrous irons and steels and the non-ferrous materials more commonly used in the submarines, including naval brasses, phosphor bronze, gunmetal, copper, aluminium, and even the more exotic materials such as lignum vitae (an extremely dense wood).

The variety of machine tools was equally surprising. There were various types of lathe, including a massive long-bed type which was used to machine ships' main shafting. Sometimes ships' shafts would become heavily scored at the bearing landings. A reclamation could often be carried out by coating the damaged area of the shaft with an Araldite mix and then using this specialized lathe to machine the repaired area back to the standard dimensions. Other lathe types included precision, capstan and numerical-controlled variations. Grinding machines, milling machines, shaping and slotting machines and drills were among the other specialist machine tools available.

None of this equipment would have been much use if skilled men had not been available to operate them. Some of the machine operators had worked in this factory for ten, twenty or even thirty years, sometimes many years on the same machine, and were really top-grade machinists. Engineering drawings were usually supplied for them to work from, but they were equally happy with a thumbline sketch on the back of a fag packet, and would produce a beautifully finished end product. These old guys could make their machines work wonders.

Another major support area was the Electrical Repair

Workshops. They overhauled all the electrical motors (AC and DC) which had been removed from the boat, and had the necessary facilities to rewire and test them before they were returned and re-installed back on board. All control gear, starters and any associated equipment could be returned to an as-new condition in these workshops.

The main Boilershop did not only manufacture and repair boilers. The main services to us were to provide brackets, cabinets or cupboards, handrails, floor-decking and welding tasks. They also carried out various heat treatments, and manufactured forgings (with the Smithery). Associated with the boilermakers, the laggers would remove lagging to enable equipment to be removed to the workshops for overhaul, and re-lag it on completion of the repairs and the reinstatement of the equipment into the vessel.

By now the dangers of working in an asbestos dust contaminated area had been recognized, and appropriate precautions were taken to protect the workforce from this extreme hazard. This would usually mean closing any compartment where removal or replacement of asbestos was necessary, and only the authorized and prepared workforce could enter, until checks had been made to ensure that it was safe to re-enter.

A very important input into the repair programme was the service provided by the Coppersmiths' Centre, manufacturing new or replacement pipes to connect the various engineering systems. 'Wires' (rod templates to the same shape and length of the required pipes) would be taken on board and returned to the shop, where the new pipe would be made, flanges fitted (one end fixed and one end loose for final length adjustment on board) by welding or brazing (with the holes pre-drilled), and returned to the boat for installation. The boat's systems could not usually be flushed and tested until the last pipe was delivered and installed.

Various other support was required, depending upon the type of boat and the 'depth' of refit; but this would usually include:

- The Hose Shop, which as the name implies would provide hoses for the various services found on board the boat: steam, water, hydraulic. oil etc.
- The Fridge Shop. The main refrigeration plants would normally be overhauled in situ (on board the boat), with any smaller domestic-type units sent to the Fridge Shop for overhaul and testing.
- The Pattern Shop/Joiners. Any furniture type repairs, patterns for the production of castings, wooden partitions, shelving, and bespoke cupboards would be arranged by this centre.

The Dockyard Laboratory was available when there was a need for unusually detailed technical support, or if scientific analysis or testing was required.

The other dockyard centres would provide support as required, and contractors provided goods and services as requested.

All in all these visits helped to give me the necessary insight to the Dockyard's structure and workings, and an understanding of who did what, and where.

One of the more interesting aspects of working on the submarine equipment was that I would now be working for John (Sarge) Pattman, who had in the meantime been promoted to Inspector, and was mad. When I say mad, I don't really mean that in a derogatory way, as Sarge was a really nice bloke; he had a heart of gold (although did his best to hide it), and was conscientious to a fault. Yes, a good bloke, but mad as a box of badgers!

I'll give you a couple of examples. One morning as I got to work and was parking up, I noticed a very agitated Sarge in the car park pacing around his car and talking to himself. I went into the office building, clocked on and made my way into my place of work. After a few minutes the door flew open and Sarge stormed in. 'Get your coat on mate' he said, 'We're going up to Hale Hamilton's.' These were the West London contractors who supplied most of the High Pressure Air Controls for the weapons equipment.

'Hang on John,' I said, 'We'll need an order form and demand number, and it would be a good idea to tell them we're coming to visit.'

'No time for that old crap mate, I know what we want, come on!' Typical John.

'Well, I've got to clock off if we are leaving the Dockyard,' I explained.

'No time for that either mate, we're leaving now!' John answered, agitated, and proceeded to jostle me down towards his car. So off we shot (the phrase 'like a bat out of hell' comes to mind).

John was not a good driver. By that I mean that if he was annoyed, and that happened all the time, he would go a nice plum colour from the neck upwards, his hair would flop down over his eyes, and he would glare at his passenger while berating whoever had upset him, in a barely controlled fury. All this would happen as he was staring at his passenger, with little reference to the road ahead. He certainly frightened me; it was just like a ride at the circus on the Wall of Death.

When we got to the outskirts of London, John became unsure of his route and looked to me for inspiration. I thought it best to admit that I didn't know the way, and this did not go down well at all. For the next few miles John scowled and muttered, with the occasional barbed glance in my direction.

We eventually got to the factory and after some detailed explanations we collected the required items. Job done. But now I had the nightmare journey back to look forward to!

John also had trouble accepting delays on his store demands. On one occasion he had ordered a major assembly for the torpedo tubes with (against my advice) a very short and unrealistic delivery date. When the requested items didn't show, John asked for them to be 'chased' and the expected delivery date obtained. It transpired that there was only one of these items in store and that was earmarked for a submarine with a higher priority. Demands had been placed with the manufacturer for additional items, and they would be available in the normal expected timeframe.

Not good enough for John. Although 'his' submarine was in

refit and a lower priority, he wanted to obtain the item held in store for the other sub. John told me to contact the stores and request that the item be diverted for us at Chatham. Of course the Stores Officer refused and referred me to his boss, who also said no.

Not good enough for John, who was by this time getting really wound up and frustrated. 'Phone his boss, mate, keep going till someone will give us the go-ahead' he said. So I phoned his boss, who said no and referred me up the chain of command.

Eventually, I was speaking to a very posh voice at the other end, and I was insisting that this item must be released to us at Chatham to prevent jeopardizing our refit programme. The person at the other end listened quite patiently, and then asked me my name and rank. I explained that I was the Technical Progressman for the Weapons Section at Chatham. Silence at the other end, and then he asked 'What is a Technical Progressman?'

I felt a bit silly by now, as it was obvious that this guy had never before heard of someone so far down the food-chain. I subsequently discovered that he was in fact a Naval Commander, and he gave John P. a massive bollocking for trying to circumnavigate the stores delivery system. John behaved himself for almost two weeks!

When John Pattman was promoted to Inspector and left the Planning Office, his replacement, Dennis Osborne, arrived. Dennis was a really nice chap, a big guy, ex RAF, always cheerful and an old-fashioned gent. He hadn't been on the section long when he was involved in an incident which had us all in hysterics for weeks.

Kathy, our tea lady was in the habit of emptying the large tea-pot that she used for the office down the toilet bowl in the cubicle next door. On this particular day Dennis was halfway through a wee inside the cubicle with the door only half closed, very large Mr Cocky in hand. Kathy, in a massive hurry as usual, entered the room and threw open the toilet door while swinging the upturned teapot (half full of cold tea) towards the toilet pan, muttering to herself as usual.

Bugger! The cold tea fountain was over Dennis's cock before he had time to dodge.

Apparently he stood there open mouthed, cock in hand (now nicely mottled with the tea-leaves) in a state of shock and embarrassment, unable to move or react. Kathy was heard to say, 'Bloody hell, you silly bastard, why don't you close the door?'

In fact she lingered far too long to stare at the 'one-eyed Python', which was a thing of beauty even camouflaged with caffeine. Eventually she forced her gaze away, and dashed out of the door giggling in a highly nervous state! Dennis always got the chocolate biscuits after that.

CHAPTER 7

SPORT AND RECREATION

It wasn't all work and no play. I love to play my sports, always did. I had played table tennis since my youth club days, and still fancied myself as a good player, so when I heard that several of the workforce used to go to the No. 9 Weapons Store on St Mary's Island to play in the lunch hour, I was very interested and decided to take a look. They used to set up two tables in the stores building, and take it in turns to play each other.

I was surprised to find that the standard of play varied considerably, and that some of the players there could beat me. The guy who organized the practice sessions was Dave Randall, and he explained that they had several teams from the Weapons club which played competitive games in the league. To cut a long story short, I joined the club and we started the Weapons IV team, in Medway Table Tennis League, Division 6.

Some of the original club players at that time included Jeff Hancock, Bill Hayward, Dave Randall, Peter Broughton, Dave Riley, Ray Packham, Bert Newborough and Martin Strike.

Weapons Table Tennis Club, 1966: L-R Geoff Hancock, Bill Hayward, Dave Randall, Peter Broughton, Dave Riley, Ray Packham, Bert Newborough, Bob Smith and Martin Strike.

I played for many years, mainly in Division 2, as we won several promotions through the Divisions. I usually played with Bert Newborough, one of the real characters in the local table tennis world. I believe that when I started playing league table tennis he was over fifty years old, but very fit for his age and a very good player. We shared some great memories, not least of all of the Medway Towns Table Tennis League annual trophy presentation evenings.

The first one I went to was held in Rochester, and the guest of honour presenting the trophies was John Simpson, the Gillingham goalkeeper and a local hero at the time. I remember his words as he presented me with my trophy: 'Take good care of it, I don't give much away!'

Another of the presentation evenings provided a hilarious interlude. The event was held in the St Mary's Island Canteen in the Chatham Dockyard, and the guest of honour presenting the trophies was Jill Hammersley, the European champion at the time. By the time we were going up to collect our trophies, Bert had already received a (surprise) award, Rochester and District Table Tennis League Sportsman of the Year, and was up on the stage again for Jill to present us with the divisional winner's trophy. Jill was obviously pleased to see the old boy receive his trophy and was making the usual polite noises. Bert was in his element, accepted his trophy with a flourish and then in a conspiratorial tone, but just loud enough for us to hear said 'Thanks very much, I expect to do even better next year. By the way, you haven't got any of your old bats you don't want, have you?'

I played in the same team as Bert for many years, and I had cause to regret it one evening when we (Weapons) were playing the Elliot's team away. It is convention that the opposition assists the home team and helps to do some of the match scoring. I volunteered to score a match, not realising that Bert would be playing against his son Malcolm for the opposition. Neither Bert nor his son played an attacking shot in the first leg, just pushing the ball back to each other for 25 minutes! This was before the 'Expedite' rule, which prevents this kind of thing happening. Come to think of it, it is probably why the Expedite rule came in! Towards the end of this match, we were all praying for a quick death. To finish my reminiscing on table tennis matters, just prior to my finishing playing in the league, after nearly fifty years, I played for

The Civil Service Sports & Social Club - Lawn Tennis Section. Bob Smith is second left, back row.

The Medway Towns Table Tennis League Annual Presentation 1970/71, held in St. Mary's Canteen, Chatham Dockyard. Bert Newborough receives his Sportsman of the Year Trophy from the European Table Tennis Champion, Jill Hammersley, and asks: "Have you got any of your old Table Tennis bats that you don't want?" Dave Randall looks on and wishes he was not there!

the Riverside team and one of our new team members was Paul Newborough, Bert's grandson. Boy, did that make me feel old!

I think it would have made Bert very proud to see his son and grandson playing league table tennis, and both good players. From my point of view it was interesting to see Bert's grandson playing a very attacking game, playing smash shots at every opportunity, while Bert himself only played an attacking shot once, and that was by accident! (joke.)

Bert Newborough was also a very keen tennis player, and played for many years for the Civil Service Club. He found out that I used to play for my school team (Chatham Technical High School), and encouraged me to join the Civil Service Club, located opposite the Central Hotel on Watling Street. There were four grass courts, which were kept in good condition, and usually at weekends when I went along, a good friendly group to give you a game. Some of my table tennis group were also tennis players, including Derek Harris and Fred Best.

Again, for his age Bert was a wonderful player, and used his head and experience rather than his legs. One thing he couldn't do of course was run, so if he started to get too far in front of me in any game, I would play my trump card. When he played the ball to me I would cut it back to him with very heavy slice so that when it bounced on the other side of the net it died. Bert couldn't get in quick enough to retrieve the ball. 'You blighter!' he would say, very nearly blaspheming for Bert. I spent many happy weekend afternoons at the tennis club. Table tennis in the winter months, and lawn tennis in the summer. Happy days!

Football was my real love. We had just won the World Cup, and how I wished that I had had the talent to match the effort I was prepared to put in. However, I joined the team I was to represent for many years after the skipper, Barry 'Jock' Nicol, invited me along to one of their pre-season training sessions at Luton Rec (Recreation Ground). I discovered that I had as much talent as most of the team!

Thus I was signed on, and my illustrious football career with Red Star had begun. I played for them for many years, dragging them down through the football divisions.

Red Star was run by Jim Silver, who was quite a character. A heavy smoker (who wasn't in those days?), Jim was fairly laid back and unfortunately had a very bad stutter, so it was extremely difficult for him to give us all a thundering good bollocking when we lost heavily (which wasn't too unusual). I was a very keen player, and I'm sure I was often picked to play because I would always turn up, play anywhere on the field, and didn't complain, rather than being blessed with any outstanding ability. I would take all my football kit to work when I was working overtime on a Saturday, clock off at two o'clock and rush up to the Civil Service sports ground in time for the kick off.

The Civil Service Sports Club facilities were by this time looking decidedly tatty. The groundsman, Bill Wragg, wasn't exactly a ball of fire, and although he looked after the bowls (top priority) and to a lesser extent the tennis courts, both of which were mainly used in the summer, and therefore could be worked upon in nicer conditions, the football pitches always seemed to be too much trouble for him. If he could persuade the referees that the grounds were unfit to play on, that suited him just fine, and he would invariably try to get the matches called off, as it seemed that it was too much of an effort for him to mark out the pitches etc.

There was never any hot water available in the showers. Although the changing rooms were supposed to be kept locked when the matches were being played, several times money and valuables went missing, and it was often rumoured that Bill had not bothered to lock up. On a personal note, I used to get on quite well with Bill, and he always seemed to be friendly with me. I don't know how much of this was because my girlfriend Joy lived just up the road from Bill, so I knew where he lived!

One of the frequent away venues was the Black Lion playing fields in Gillingham (not the present day building and facilities - in the late 60s things were much more primitive). The original changing rooms had no showers; instead a large bath which could accommodate about ten men was the post-match washing facility. This was OK, but there were several pitches, and as the games were played simultaneously, after matches it was first come, first served. Needless to say the water was not changed until the matches had finished and all the players had bathed and changed. In consequence, if you were the last team to finish your match and get into the bath, it looked just like mulligatawny soup!

We were usually late kicking off, for as I often said at the time we were the only team I knew that could get tired out just getting changed for a match!

We kicked off late, so we finished our matches late, and were left with the mulligatawny soup option, if you were that desperate.

Some memories of matches stay with you forever. I remember one when we played 'Strand' (Athletic I believe), at the Black Lion playing fields. The Strand were known at this time to be a bit 'basic' (they would kick you rather than the ball if they got the chance).

On this day they had the two Simmons brothers playing, and both were obviously pissed at kick-off. We scored twice in a very untidy first half, so the Simmons boys decided to try a little intimidation. They kicked us off the pitch in the second half, and after being verbally cautioned (but not booked) they started to abuse the referee. I hadn't seen that degree of blatant abuse of a referee before, and haven't since; effing and blinding wasn't in it, it was right in the ref's face. He seemed completely out of his depth, and I doubt if he ever refereed another match in his life! We lost the match, by the way.

Another match I remember well, was when I scored TWO goals in one match. (Not own goals, although I was pretty good at those.) I had given up smoking (again) about three weeks before, and really felt that the benefits were starting to show. My breathing seemed much easier, and I felt as if I could run all day (mostly psychological of course). Anyway, the first goal was a 20-yard lob over the keeper's head and the second was a left-foot shot (yes, left foot, the one I don't kick with) all along the ground when we were pressurizing at a corner. I still have the newspaper cutting! We won 3-2. I was that excited I went to the pub that night to celebrate with my mate Ted Arnold, and after a few pints I decided that a celebratory cigar wouldn't affect my no smoking situation. Wrong. After three cigars that night I was back on the smoking again. A bad move.

A show-stopping episode never seen on 'Match of the Day' happened when we (the defence) complained to the forwards that they were not holding onto the ball when it was cleared from the defence. This meant it was continually coming back to us, until eventually the opposition scored, through constant pressure.

'For Christ's sake keep hold of the ball and give us a break at the back!' pleaded our centre-half, Barry Harris.

'Huh! Think you can do any better?' was the response from our centre-forward.

'Yes, I bloody well can, and I'll show you, we'll swap positions for the second half and I'll go up front', replied Barry. And so the die was set.

Barry was a stocky centre-half, and all our football kit was medium size. I mention this because his shorts in particular didn't fit him too well. They were far too small. This didn't matter too much when he was playing at centre-half, as his running was mainly restricted to ten-yard blocking runs and heading out high balls. Playing at centre-forward was altogether different.

About 10 minutes into the second half, one of us defenders sent a long ball to our (new) centre-forward Barry. He caught the ball on his chest and started on a determined run towards the opposition's goal, brushing aside one or two defenders as he went. As he got to the opposition's penalty area, we noticed that their keeper was laughing - not just a giggle but a full-bloodied rib-hugging guffaw. With their keeper temporarily and mysteriously incapacitated, now was our big chance to score. Go on Barry, hammer it in!

He did. It missed, and the ball flew way over their bar.

Now we had the time to check on the strange behaviour of the opposition's keeper.

What had made him laugh so much, we enquired?

'Look at his shorts!' the keeper replied, pointing at Barry and still hooting. We all looked at Barry's shorts and saw that because they were so inadequate, during his extended run they had allowed his cock to escape, and it was protruding from the bottom of his shorts. Bloody hell! Quite frightening, even for us, and we had seen it all before in the showers.

The keeper, still giggling, managed to explain. 'When I saw you steaming in at me in goal, I wasn't sure if you were going to have a shot or try to put a good fuck into me' he said.

Enough said, how do you follow that?

I also used to play on Sunday mornings, friendly matches for Wigmore. These were all away matches, as we had no home venue, and we mostly played pub teams in villages around Maidstone. Bob Webb, a pal from schooldays, and another friend, Brian Jackson, a diver in the Dockyard, were two of the regulars in the Sunday team. Two of the teams we played on a regular basis were the Duke of Wellington at Ryarsh and a team from Hadlow, where it always seemed to take forever to get there. These matches were great fun. They were not taken too seriously, but were more of a good workout and a pleasant way to get rid of last night's beer.

CHAPTER 8

PART OF THE TEAM

I had now been doing the Technical Progressman job for a couple of years and I felt I was really contributing to the section's output. I now understood how the naval Stores system worked (where items were held, which forms were used to demand and return items etc) and where to source the items which were to be made locally. I had worked hard, even if I say so myself, to learn and to improve my working skills, and it was paying off. The difficult problems and tensions of my earlier days were a thing of the past. I had settled in, was doing a good job, and I was well liked and popular. Not to say modest, of course!

The production officers recognized that I had now acquired the necessary skills, and could be relied upon to provide the assistance they required. It was still a learning process, which was as it should be, but I now felt that I was fully trained. Having said that, we still looked to extend our knowledge and have a bit of fun at the same time. One of the other Progressmen (Harry Rogers, or HT as he was known), had joined the Planning Office recently. The two of us used to quiz each other on knowledge of the Naval Stores class/group references. All equipment held in the Naval Stores has a unique reference number which comprises a four-figure class/group, eg 0269 would be a bearing

(Ball or Roller), and it would be followed by the pattern number, eg 914-0627. So the conversation would go something like:

Me: 'OK Harry, what is Naval Stores Class/Group 0269?'

HT: 'Ball and Roller bearings. OK Smithy, What is Naval Stores Class/Group 0212?'

Me: 'Nuts, Bolts, and Fastenings.'

HT: 'OK - What is Naval Stores Class/Group 0413?'

Me: 'Ebonite Quills and Rubber Goods.'

We always found this one highly amusing. (What do they say about little things pleasing little minds?)

At about this time several vacancies occurred for Chargeman (Technical Supervisor), which later evolved into the Professional and Technology Officer Grade IV, the first line management role. The Dockyard Personnel Department decided to invite interested volunteers to attend a selection interview, and I was encouraged to go. I attended the interview and remember that Johnny Bubb and Ron Barnes were two of the three Board members on the interview panel.

I can still remember that one of the interview questions was 'What material is EN57?' (Answer: it's a corrosion-resisting steel, a type of stainless.)

I passed the interview, and while I waited for a permanent vacancy to occur, was invited to do Deputy Chargeman duties in the Weapons Section. This was to cover for annual leave and sick leave, and other periods of absence by the permanent chargemen, and would provide me with invaluable experience for when I took up my permanent post on promotion.

My first period of 'cover' was for Eric Carter, the Chargeman in the Weapons Annexe section. Eric was a nice old boy; he must have been well over 60 years old at this time (which seemed ancient to me), slightly built and quietly spoken.

Harry Barnett had taken over from Peter Lowry as the Chargeman in the Planning Office, not, we were told, anything to do with Pete's band-playing antics, but more due to the fact that Harry had suffered heart trouble, and it was thought that the Planning Office would provide a less stressful working environment. Anyway, Harry had a word in my 'shell like' when he knew I was going to do deputy for Eric Carter. He explained that Eric was not really very interested in the planning returns that were required weekly by the Planning Office, and preferred to continue with his own system. As he was so near to retirement, no one wanted to harass him, so his planning returns were 'guesstimated' by the Planning Office. Harry said he wanted me to get the proper returns done, without upsetting Eric too much, while I was deputising.

Before he went on leave, I asked Eric if I could change things a little to make it easier for me, and he readily agreed. Then I did as I was told, and rearranged the work cards into the (previously unused) loading boxes, which showed which work each man on the section was working on, and of course from this you could work out how much work was still to be done - the principle of work loading. This made the completion of the section workload reports that the Planning Office needed easy to complete.

The receipt of these long-awaited report forms delighted

Harry in the Planning Office; however his joy was short-lived. When Eric returned from his leave, I explained in great detail what I had done and how easy it was to fill in the required forms. He listened very patiently and nodded sagely from time to time. He seemed quite impressed, and thanked me for taking care of the section in his absence. 'Do you think that you will be all right to do these returns now Eric?' I asked. 'No problems, young man,' was his reassuring reply.

I felt quite pleased that my first period in substitution had gone so well. The paperwork side of the job was in place and up to date, and the supervisory duties had proved very interesting. This may have been helped by the fact that I knew two of the fitters very well, Bob Webb and Len Harris, who were usually employed refitting the Reavall TC4 air compressors used in the subs.

About four weeks later Eric took some more leave and I was asked to deputise again. When I went down to the section for the handover, I found that he had reverted to his old 'system'. There were workcards everywhere, no apparent system or logic (to me anyway), and only he knew how he worked it. But perhaps that was the object of the exercise? Oh well, c'est la vie!

My next period of substitution cover was for Ned Foster, the Chargeman of the Main Shop. The most high profile task in the Main Shop was the refit of the ships' main armament, the 4.5" Mk 6 gun mountings. These massive assemblies can be quite an awe-inspiring sight, not only for their size and complexity, but because they are just like an iceberg - most of the mounting cannot be seen as it is usually underground, being mounted over large purpose-designed pits. The two fitters who refitted most of these mountings were Les Taylor and Freddy Whale; they had worked on these assemblies over many years and become expert. This was probably the only piece of kit that could equal the submarine equipment in terms of priority and importance, which was reflected when stores were demanded or materials ordered. A higher than normal delivery code could be used and would usually be accepted and achieved.

Freddy and Les initially seemed to me to be quite aloof and reluctant to join in with the day-to-day happenings in the workshop, but when I did the chargehand duties it soon became clear that they were always helpful and ready to advise if asked. It was just that they preferred to get on with their work in hand and were happy to concentrate on that. That was probably what made them so reliable and efficient.

The 4.5" Gun mounting is a very complex piece of kit, and extensive test equipment is required, especially for the gun's hydraulic system. Purpose-built hydraulic system filtration packs are used to flush the warmed hydraulic oil continually until the acceptable degree of purity is achieved.

At the east end of the main workshop was a discrete area known as the dustproof room. This area contained a back projection microscope which was used to view the size of any contamination particles found in the hydraulic oil, taken regularly from test points during the flushing process. A clean examination area was essential for these and other tests. Other critical tests checked for backlash and gear engagement loads in the guns' gearboxes.

Other guns were refitted in the workshop as well. The main 'bread and butter' gun was the 40mm Mk 7, a twin Bofors gun used for anti-aircraft and close range defence roles. The Mk 7 was a hydraulically-operated unit; other variants in service at this time being the Mk 8, a battery-operated version, and the Mk 9, electrically operated. These two variants however were rarer and tended to be used in specialist roles.

The other gun mounting we overhauled in the workshop on a regular basis at this time was the Oerlikon 20mm, a very simple twin-barrelled gun. Although quite dated, they were found to be very useful to the Navy for close range protection, particularly when the larger armaments could not depress sufficiently to fire at very close range targets, eg to deter small, usually fast craft from attacking.

Several of the support trades were usually in attendance in the workshop, and a significant part of my duties was to ensure that they were not held up in doing their tasks, that they knew which tasks we required of them, when they were required, and that they had been requisitioned to do this work. This was where I would learn my basic liaison and communication skills.

The main assist trades included the boilermakers, who had a small workshop area dedicated to them. They would supply us with brackets, handrails, machine seatings, any steel or aluminium platework that was required, and welding tasks if necessary.

Electricians, although not in constant attendance, would be removing original equipment for transport to the Electrical Workshop for repairs and reinstalling and testing these items as they were returned. This would chiefly be electric motors, starters, control gear lighting and instrument panels.

Coppersmiths also played an important part in the refits. Old pipework was removed and taken to their workshop (or the PIP shop) for cleaning and test; any damaged or broken pipework or that failing testing would be replaced. New and refurbished pipes were annealed (stress removed and softened) if required, prior to replacement within the gun mounting. The majority of the pipework was for the hydraulic, lubricating oil, air and cooling water systems.

At the west end of the main workshop were the Limited Working Stock Store ('The Stores') and the Loan Tool Store. The stores held, among other items, all the consumable supplies which would be required during the refit process. These included nuts, bolts, washers, various jointing materials (Permanite and oil and water jointing, insertion rubber and cork sheets etc), 'O' seals, sprays, polishes, oils greases, grease guns, liquid measures, labels, string, cleaning rags, emery papers and consumable tools such as files, knives and hacksaw blades.

The Loan Tool Store situated next door held the large, expensive, specialized or unusual equipment (including some test sets, general purpose and specialised) which would be used intermittently during the refit. These items were 'drawn out' for a specific task and returned to the Loan Tool Store on completion.

A card showing all the equipment details and serial numbers would be signed by the workman, who would also give his works number when he drew and returned the kit. This system also ensured that the items when returned into the store were checked and/or tested to ensure that they were always in a serviceable condition and ready for re-issue.

These stores were known as 'controlled items'. These special items, or controlled stores, would vary depending upon which equipment was being refitted, but would usually include such items as special spanners (usually in boxed sets), torque wrenches, unusual taps and dies, extractors and test-pumps and gauges.

Completing the store setup was the Weapons Equipment Store. This was located on a mezzanine floor adjacent to the Afloat Chargeman's office. This store held the weapons-specific store items (spare parts). Full details of these items would be held within the Stock Control Office.

Located below the mezzanine floor was the drying room, a heated room where clothes and overalls could be dried out, for workmen coming to work, returning from working outside or on board the ship or submarine.

Last but not least, opposite the clocking-in station was the office of the Trade Union Convener, Fred Foster. Fred was a very popular member of the team. This was mainly because of his very friendly and cheerful personality, his 'go the extra mile' efforts to champion his members' causes and perhaps most importantly, his common-sense approach. He was well respected by the management team, and very popular with his Trade Union members.

One of the real characters I now came across was Pete

Rowlands. Pete was a labourer in the workshop, and was unfortunate enough to be cursed with learning difficulties. When he got excited he used to bark: it was a very good impression of a large dog. He would be walking through the main shop and suddenly burst into a loud 'WOOF, WOOF, WOOF'! This took a bit of getting used to, but after a while the regular workforce hardly noticed it any more. However it was quite amusing to see the look on visitors' faces when it happened. Incidentally Pete was as strong as an ox, and a very good worker.

I found my first period as Chargehand in the main shop without problems, very interesting and enjoyable, and not at all as daunting as I had first imagined, due in no small part to the willingness and helpful attitude of the workforce in the section.

I returned to the Planning Office to resume my normal duties and to tidy up the problems that had been carried over during my absence. It was at about this time that Don Rousell joined the Planning Office as a colleague doing progressman duties and taking over the submarine work. Don lived in Faversham and came up on the train every morning, which meant a very early start and probably explained why he always looked shagged out. He did however have a wicked sense of humour, which would explain in part why we got on so well. Don liked to go fishing, usually on the coast near his home (Faversham or Whitstable), and as I was very keen at this time also, we always had a few fishermen's tales to relate.

Don's real love of his life was his sailing. He owned a catamaran which he raced, and was very successful locally. If he had had a good weekend's racing, and sometimes even if not, he would relate in humorous terms the weekend's boating activities. He always made it sound very interesting, with tales of meeting loads of new and existing friends, and it was obviously very exciting out on the water seeing the local coastline from another perspective.

On several occasions he had suggested I might like to crew for him, and as he made it sound so exciting and out of the usual, I was almost at the point of accepting; I was only reluctant because I was not a strong swimmer. Then he brought the photos in. Shit! The crew member was on the hull, which was way out of the water, about four or five feet I would guess, and judging by the wake the boat was creating they were doing a considerable speed.

I noticed also that the crewman seemed to have rather a strange look on his face, as if he was trying to decide if he had just shit himself, and if he was ever going to get to the shore in one piece! I declined the offer to go crewing.

We did organize the occasional office nights out between ourselves. This wasn't easy because of the geographical spread of our homes. The one night that comes most easily to mind was when Don organized a trip to his local (well almost local), the Shipwright's Arms at Oare.

What Don forgot to tell us was that the landlady, Mrs Tester, used to like a drink or three, and when she had had a drink she would often come around into the bar and get *very* friendly with the customers. This night when she came to the other side of the bar she made a beeline for Ron Hill. Ron was one of the Estimators in our office, probably in his mid forties, very quietly spoken, inoffensive and appeared almost shy. Mrs Tester pounced. She sat on Ron's lap and proceeded to twirl his non-existent curls (Ron was very bald). She appeared to be whispering sweet nothings in his ear, and was obviously in a state of near delirium. Ron wasn't. I don't think he quite knew what to do. Should he push her off his lap and chance being rude? No - that wouldn't do. Should he let her 'get on with it'? No, that wouldn't do either.

He was by this stage fully embarrassed, and glowing a beautiful pink. Don, on the other hand - he had organized the night out remember - was giggling fit to burst. He had spilt half of his pint laughing —served him right!

Ron was eventually saved by the arrival of the landlord. Initially his arrival looked as if it might be a mixed blessing; how would he, the landlord, react to the interesting spectacle before him? No problem, he had obviously seen it all before. He instructed his wife to 'stop pestering the customers' and see who needed serving in the saloon bar. Surprisingly, Mrs Tester prised herself off Ron, gave him a 'thank you very much' smile and headed off to the saloon.

Phew! Ron breathed a big sigh of relief, and so did we - she might have pounced on any of us! The rest of the evening was quiet. Well, how do you follow that?

Only a couple of weeks later, I was asked to do the Deputy Chargeman duties in the PIP Shop. The 'top man' in the shop was Norman Peters. Norman was over six feet tall, perhaps in his mid-forties, with lots of black hair swept back and Brylcreemed into place and a lively demeanour. He was very keen on sport (I believe he could have been ex Army), and kept himself very fit by cycling to work. He effectively ran the place. Second-in-command was Percy Wheeler, a few years older than Norman; he had worked in the shop for many years, knew the place inside out, and despite having a very bad club foot was highly mobile. The other guys were fairly anonymous; didn't say too much, just got on with their jobs.

The PIP shop stank. The de-greasing, de-painting and de-rusting processes required industrial strength cleaners. Although normally the large double doors, the main entry and exit were left open, this was insufficient to vent the acrid stench created by the huge tanks of powerful cleaning chemicals. A couple of small extraction fans paid lip-service to fume extraction, but to deal adequately with this environment a dedicated and powerful fume extraction system would have been required.

I suspect that in the early days of the workshop when the cleaning systems were different, and probably also the layout of the shop and the chemicals used, it had been OK, but now it certainly was not. Over the years the chemical cleaning tanks had been enlarged (to accommodate larger assemblies), steam heating coils had been fitted into most of the tanks (to heat the chemicals and make them more effective, and at the same time soften the contamination to be removed), and much more powerful chemicals were now being used. This is not intended as a direct criticism of the management team, as this situation (like so many others) evolved gradually, with small changes one at a time, until the present unsatisfactory situation was arrived at. No one had the time or inclination to look back to the original concept. The present setup worked very well, the cleaning process being to a very high standard, and no one complained about the conditions (too much) - what, and lose the overtime?

So conditions were largely ignored. The present layout housed the large steam-heated tanks, usually one containing Ardrox, and the other Tricoethylene. As an attempt to minimize the generation of fumes into the atmosphere these tanks were topped with what looked like large table-tennis balls completely covering and floating on top of the liquid cleaner. They helped, but not much.

Two more large tanks were sited almost alongside. The first was a hot water bath, which finished the cleaning process, removing the odd particles of grease, paint flakes or whatever. The last tank was empty, but was used with a powerful water lance to flush all the remaining cleaning chemicals from the cleaned assemblies. This tank could also be used with paraffin to brush off small items which were lightly contaminated, and then to use the water jets to rinse them clean.

Benches located around the work areas held the materials for their specific tasks. Along one side was an area which held all the large rolls of 'mouldable wrap' (a heavy duty type of synthetic cloth impregnated with an oily substance), with which items were wrapped before additional layers of preservation/packaging were added. Next was an area storing large rolls of polythene sheets used to manufacture heavy duty packing bags, and with them were a couple (one large, one small) of heat-sealing machines.

Along the opposite side of the workshop, large quantities of corrugated cardboard sheets were stacked. These were used for the manufacture of cardboard packing boxes of all shapes and sizes. A folding machine used for the manufacture of the boxes was positioned nearby.

At the end were two printing machines, one a printing machine proper which was used to manufacture the identification labels secured to the packaged item, and also on the box or package that it came in. The other was really an embosser, used to create metal printed labels used on packing cases etc.

Stored on shelves along both sides were various other materials used in the packaging process. These included nylon twine, string, brown sticky paper reels, pre-printed labels and bags of desiccant (silica gel), a substance put in with a packaged item to absorb moisture, thereby keeping the packaged item 'dry' and preventing corrosion and deterioration.

The layout was completed by a tiny office for the Chargeman (desk, chair, cupboard, and phone) and a small 'rest room' where the workforce could eat their sandwiches, with access to a small oven for heating tins of soup, pies etc.

Saturdays (overtime) were a special day. Norman would offer to cook a bacon-and-egg breakfast for anyone who wanted it. I was flattered to be asked, and very grateful, but somehow I could not face eating bacon and egg (even if it was my favourite) in that place, in those conditions. No, the smell put me right off; not for me. However, most of the others enjoyed it, so good luck to them.

Saturday overtime was usually to cope with the work demand; in other words not all the work that had to be done could be completed in the normal working week. Bear in mind that most of the work in the PIP shop was process related, and had to be completed in a finite time. For example large items might require eight hours soaking in the cleaning agent tanks to soften and remove the paint/grease/rust so they could be returned to as-new and clean condition.

So Saturday overtime was used to catch-up with the backlog. Approximately every six weeks however, the cleaning tanks had to be drained, cleaned and replenished with new chemicals. The interval would obviously depend upon the usage in that period. On these Saturdays the shop would be closed for normal production work, and this and other maintenance tasks would take precedence. Stock levels, ordering of materials and servicing of the equipment were organized to be synchronized to these 'down days'. The Yard Services 'gang' would be requested to attend, and do their servicing to the steam traps on the heating system and the cleaning tanks and any other maintenance or testing that was due. The electrical items were treated in the same way, checks and maintenance being done on the electric motors and the lighting.

One of the problems I experienced as the Deputy Chargeman in the PIP shop was how to respond to the frequent requests for 'rabbits'. A 'rabbit' is the Dockyard term for private jobs intended for home, sometimes called 'homers'. Unfortunately the PIP shop was a gold mine for items and services that were in great demand, and I hadn't been told what to expect in the way of the frequent requests.

It soon became clear that the cleaning tanks were very popular with motor and motorbike enthusiasts, to get their components all new and shiny, as well as gardening types with their mowers, guys who had boats and scores of other people who wanted some item or other properly cleaned.

Other requests were for supplies of the nylon line (ideal for fishing I was told), polythene sheets (greenhouses?) and various printing requests. The PIP shop had supplies of various coloured papers and excellent printing facilities. It could even professionally scroll or provide 'teeth-edge' surrounds on tickets and invitation cards - very handy!

My personal thoughts were that it was all a matter of degree. If someone wanted a small job done for themselves, there was no profit motive, and he did not keep coming back, I thought it was probably OK. However some of the request were just taking the piss.

I had a quiet word with Norman, for advice really, and told him how I felt about the situation. His reaction was commonsense and to the point. He explained that most of the unofficial requests didn't come through me (I didn't see them, as the requester went direct to the workman, often when I was out of the workshop) and the workforce had enough sense and experience to keep these enterprises under control by refusing most of them. He suggested that I should refuse all except a few 'genuine' requests. Good advice, I thought. The thin end of the wedge is the one you usually miss!

I really enjoyed the time I spent as the Deputy Chargeman in the PIP shop, in spite of the obnoxious working environment, which always left me with a sense of unease. What were all these acrid fumes doing to our insides, on a day-by-day basis? However, I was only on duty in this section for short deputizing periods, so hopefully any damage would be minimal. With that reservation, the job was great. The team were motivated and conscientious, and accepted me without reservation; I believe they recognised that it was my intention to help them maintain the excellent support they provided, and they responded accordingly.

I had now attended courses on Network Scheduling and Planning Tools, including PERT (Programme Evaluation and Review Technique), pie charts, ghant (bar) charts and simple logic diagrams. These systems were invaluable for complex activities, eg a nuclear submarine refit, where literally hundreds of activities would be happening either simultaneously or in quick succession to each other, and it was vitally important to identify problems and delays to ensure early and quick remedial actions.

With the simpler activities commonplace in the Dockyard, less complex and easier systems to manage were better suited to the normal tasks. The basic tool of the overall planning system was the 'Section Workload Report'. This simple system listed the work packages in an approximate priority, and showed the total number of hours allocated to complete the work.

The number of operators (fitters/labourers/others) was multiplied by the net hours in the working week. If 40 hours were worked (gross) in the week, an allowance had to be made for 'diversions' (things such as union meetings, first aid lectures etc), so a figure of 35 would probably be used. Therefore, the work package hours would be divided by 35 and loaded in successive weeks until the project was completed. As the section capacity was known (number of men x 35), each week could be loaded to the known figure. The main advantages of this scheme of course, were that it could demonstrate the need for additional staff or overtime to complete jobs, or conversely identify periods when extra work would be required to keep the section fully employed.

I personally had no problems at all working with the system, and found it to be an extremely valuable management tool. Having said that, I must confess that I was already a convert to the need for a simple but effective planning system, almost from day one. However, some of my peers, and certainly a significant percentage of the older first line managers, viewed the inception of planning systems with major reservations. This, I believe, was primarily for three reasons:

Firstly, I think a lot of the older supervisors saw the introduction of a planning system as an erosion of their control over the work done in their section, and the requirement for them to make weekly formal reports worried them.

Secondly, the philosophy behind the introduction of the planning requirement was not adequately explained, before the systems were implemented.

The last reason was that financial control was now dramatically changing the way the dockyards operated. Financial returns were now a way of life, and caused considerable headaches for the production boys, who had to change their ways, making cases for funding, and showing value for money. Now that planning feedback was to be required, it seemed to be another needless task required by departments detached from the 'sharp end'. In other words, the planners were seen to be tarred with the same brush as the (perceived) useless Finance Branch. (No help, just a hindrance to the production staff.)

As I said, this was not my understanding at all; I found that by effective planning, vital assistance could be offered to the production teams. This fostered real teamwork, and together we got the boats out in time. This achievement should not be underestimated, as Chatham Dockyard was invariably proven to be able to refit the warships put in its charge not only to time, but to cost and to quality. This, I would suggest, made life a lot easier for the Royal Navy, and made a significant contribution to the defence of the realm.

About six months after my successful Chargeman's interview, my name had reached the top of the 'awaiting promotion' list, and I was offered a permanent post as the Technical Supervisor (the new name for the Chargemen) on the Outstations section of the Yard Services Department. I was sorry to leave the Weapons Section and all the friends I had made there, but I knew it was time for a move, and this promotion was a good opportunity for me to pursue my ambitions and secure my future.

So, heavy hearted, I left the Weapons Section in October 1968 and took up my new post with the Yard Services Department. But that's another story…

THE CAST

Weapons Section, HM Dockyard, Chatham, circa 1966

Commander 'G' - Cmdr (RN) Harding.

Foremen: Vic Bennett, Ken Lovell, Foreman Weapons Afloat (FWA) and Shops (FWS).

Inspectors: Ted Baker, Ron Collins, Arthur Regan, Frank Stevens. Peter Biddle, Fred Kimmings, Bill Carden, John Patman were all later.

Chargemen: Charlie Adams, Harry Barnett, Alec Bond, Ken Brockwell, Eric Carter,

Ned Foster, Pete Lowry, Phil Hobling, Bill Stevens (also Trade Union Official)

Fitters: Bob Webb, Lenny Price, Len Harris, Bob Moncur, Fred Whale, Les Taylor, John Peters, Rod Berwick, Peter Castle, Roy Beard, Ernie Holden, Barry Harris, Brian Turner, Ted Robinson, Ken Oliver and Trevor Sergeant.

PIP Shop: Norman Peters and Percy Wheeler.

Planning Office: Estimators; Jim Greenaway, Norman Shipley, Dennis Osborne, Jack Payne, Ron Hill, John Pattman (before promotion) Horry Wood (later).

Progressmen (Technical): Ken Hancock, Fred Murr, Keith Harris, Bob Butler and Bob Smith; Don Rousell and Harry Rogers (both later).

Progressmen (Non-Technical): Ted Broady and Bill Allen.

Stock Control Office: Jack Taylor + 2 clerical assistants.

Stores Officer: Len Parfitt.

Trade Union (AUEW) Convener: Fred Foster.

Technical Library: Fred Ludlow.

Diagnosticians: Ted Coward, Wally Mason, Charlie Swan.

And most importantly: The Tea Lady, Kathy Cook.

Apologies to all those not mentioned above.